QUESTIONS PENTECOSTALS ASK

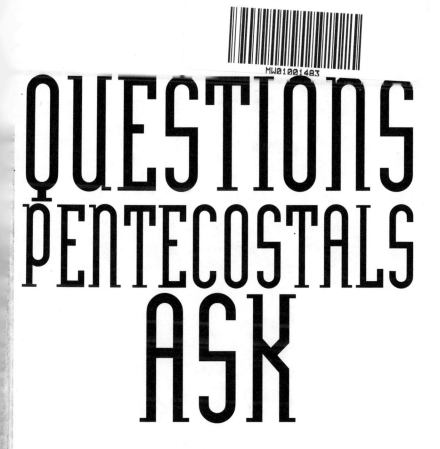

QUESTIONS
PENTECOSTALS
ASK

DAVID F. GRAY

Questions Pentecostals Ask
By David F. Gray

©1987 Word Aflame Press
Hazelwood, MO 63042-2299
Reprint History: 1987, 1990, 1992, 1995, 2000

Cover Design by Paul Povolni

All Scripture quotations in this book are from the King James Version of the Bible unless otherwise identified. Some Scripture quotations from *The Amplified* ©1965 by Zondervan Publishing House used by permission. Some verses from *The Living Bible*, copyright 1971 by Tyndale House Publishers, Wheaton, IL. Used by permission. Scripture quotations from the *New American Standard Bible.* ©The Lockman Foundation 1960, 1962, 1963, 1968, 1971, 1972, 1973, 1975, 1977 used by permission.

WORD AFLAME®PRESS
8855 DUNN ROAD
HAZELWOOD, MO 63042-2299

Library of Congress Cataloging-in-Publication Data

Gray, David F., 1917—
  Questions Pentecostals ask.

  Originally appeared in a question and answer column in Gospel Tidings,
  Includes indexes.
  1. United Pentecostal Church—Doctrines—Miscellanea.
2. Pentecostal churches—Doctrines—Miscellanea.
3. Christian life—Pentecostal authors—Miscellanea.
I. Gospel Tidings (Modesto, Calif.) II. Title.
BX8780.G73   1986   230'.994   86-26784
ISBN 0-932581-07-2

Table of Contents

Foreword

Reverend David F. Gray is a minister whom I have esteemed and honored for many years. As a small child, I looked to Reverend Gray as a true example of both a Christian and a minister. Many times, my father, who was a young minister, sought the advice and counsel of Brother Gray. He always answered with love, wisdom, scriptural knowledge, meekness and consistency. These attributes are still prevalent in the ministry of Brother Gray today.

It was because of these godly qualities that the Western District Board of the United Pentecostal Church International asked him to serve as associate editor of the *Gospel Tidings* and to write the "Question and Answer" column which appears monthly. Brother Gray has served faithfully and honorably in this capacity for many years. His love, wisdom, and scriptural backing when answering questions in the *Gospel Tidings* have been a tremendous blessing to our constituency.

As editor of the *Gospel Tidings,* it was my honor and pleasure to work in unity with him. I feel it was inspiration from God that prompted Brother Gray to compile in book form the "Questions and Answers" which have appeared for several years in the *Gospel Tidings*. This is a book which needs to be in every Christian home.

May your life and spirituality be enriched and perfected as you read and study this book.

Reverend Leonard D. Sansom
Former editor of *Gospel Tidings*

Introduction

Reverend David F. Gray, a man of great integrity, stands giant tall in that elect number of "the tried and faithful."

From vast experience and keen knowledge gleaned from a Spirit-filled ministry, he has shared with us scriptural answers to numerous puzzling questions of life.

You will be the enlightened reaper as you ponder over his storehouse of understanding. He presents Jesus as Lord and Master of every facet of life.

This book contains the accumulation of questions sent by inquirers and the answers God has inspired Reverend Gray to give over a period of years as he authored the question and answer column in the monthly publication, *Gospel Tidings.*

May new vistas of broadened visions and wisdom be yours as you strengthen or add to your understanding by Brother Gray's positive approach to complex areas of today's living.

Reverend Paul R. Price
Superintendent of the Western District,
United Pentecostal Church International

1
Doctrinal Points

The Term "Jesus Only"

QUESTION:

Would you please tell me what ministers mean when they say we are "Jesus Only"?

ANSWER:

I am sure many of those who use this expression are fine, sincere, and godly people. I do not for one moment doubt their good intentions and sincerity, but I personally feel that it is an unwise and misleading statement. Using unscriptural expressions such as this tends to turn people away before they have a chance to hear the truth.

While there is some truth in the statement, it is only a half-truth. Was there a God before Bethlehem? Of course. Then God existed before He ever came to us as Jesus to save and redeem us. In other words, Jesus was God, but God was not always manifested as Jesus.

And too, we are giving ammunition to our enemies when we use this phrase, for they will say, "See, those 'Jesus Only' people do not believe in the fatherhood of God everywhere taught in Scripture, nor in the Holy Ghost." This is absolutely untrue! We believe wholeheartedly in the fatherhood of God and in the manifestation of God as the Holy Ghost.

When we use statements such as "Jesus Only," people who know their Bibles and who otherwise would come in and accept the truth are turned away because of the manifest absurdity. It is not necessary to use phrases which cause our precious doctrine to be misunderstood and needlessly rejected.

We should strive to use scriptural expressions, those with which we shall "be able by sound doctrine both to exhort and to convince the gainsayers" (Titus 1:9).

··············

The Father and the Son

QUESTION:

How can you say there is only one person in God, when Revelation 5:1-7 tells us that the Lamb (Jesus) took the book out of the hand of Him that sat on the throne (God the Father)? In John 17:11 Jesus prayed to the Father "that they (His disciples) may be one as we are." When a man and a woman get married they become one, but they are still two persons. Jesus and God are one, but two persons, God and the Son of God, which together with the Holy Spirit make up the Holy Trinity.

ANSWER:

I do not think you realize how full of contradictions your letter is. For instance, you say that Jesus (the Son of God) and God are two persons in a trinity of divine persons making up the Godhead. The Trinity doctrine states that these three are "co-equal, co-existent, and co-eternal." Yet in the Scripture you quoted (John 17:11), we have (according to your teaching) one divine person or God praying to another divine person or God. Why would He have to pray to another God if He were God in His own right? The one praying must certainly be less powerful than the one prayed to, so evidently you believe you have a little God and a big God; yet Jesus said, "All power is given unto me in heaven and in earth" (Matthew 28:18). Therefore He must be the only God that has any power!

Now, what did Jesus mean when He prayed in John 17:11, "That they may be one as we are?" He explained it in verses 21 and 23: "That they all may be one; as thou, Father, art in me, and I in thee, that they may be one in us. . .I in them, and thou in me, that they also may be made perfect in one. . . ." The way we are made one is for us to partake of the same Spirit by Jesus coming into us, "I in them." This is what happens when we receive the Holy Ghost.

Jesus said in John 14:16: "And I will pray the Father, and he shall give you another Comforter, that he may abide with you for ever." Immediately Jesus explained who this Comforter is by saying that He is "the Spirit of truth" (John 14:17). It can be none other than the Spirit of Jesus Himself, for He said in verse 6 that He was the truth! So that none could mistake that He was speaking of Himself coming back to dwell in them when the Holy Ghost came, He said, "I will not leave you comfortless (mg. 'orphans'); I will come to you " (verse 18). And finally He declared in verse 20: "At that day [when the Holy Ghost comes in], ye shall know that I am in my Father, and ye in me, and I in you."

That is the oneness that Jesus prayed for in John 17! We are made one by the same Spirit, Christ Himself filling us and making us one in Him.

"For as the body is one, and hath many members, and all the members of that one body,

> *being many, are one body: so also is Christ. For*
> *by one Spirit are we all baptized into one body. . ."*
> *(I Corinthians 12:12-13).*

You may ask why Jesus then described the Spirit as "another Comforter" in John 14:16, if it was Christ Himself who was to come into them. Simply because when He came back at Pentecost He did not want them to expect to see Him as they saw Him then—in a body of flesh—yet He wanted them to know that the Spirit they were to receive was truly Himself, come in *another* form, in Spirit-form.

It is true that husband and wife are one, but no husband can say, "He that hath seen me hath seen my wife." Yet Jesus said, "He that hath seen me hath seen the Father " (John 14:9). So the oneness of God in Christ is certainly not the same as that of a husband and wife.

Now let us look at Revelation 5. The key to the understanding of this account is to discover who the One on the throne is. There was only One on the throne (Revelation 4:2), who is identified as "the Lord God Almighty which was, and is, and is to come" (Revelation 4:8). That this is Jesus cannot be denied: "Behold he cometh with clouds. . .I am Alpha and Omega. . .saith the Lord, which is, and which was, and which is to come, the Almighty" (Revelation 1:7-9); "I am Alpha and Omega. . .I Jesus. . ." (Revelation 22:13, 16). Therefore the One on the throne is none other than Jesus in His deity, which is the Almighty.

Since the One on the throne is Jesus, then who is the Lamb? Notice the Lamb came from the midst of the throne (Revelation 5:6), a perfect example of God leaving His glory and being made flesh. "He who sat upon the throne" was our Lord Jesus Christ as the Almighty God, while the Lamb is Jesus the Son of God who was slain. This then is a graphic picture of both the deity and the humanity of Christ.

Undoubtedly objections will be raised that Jesus could not be both the One on the throne and the Lamb who came out of the midst of the throne. Why not? In the very same context He is both the Lion and the Lamb. In John 10 Jesus is both the Shepherd, the Door to the sheepfold, and the Lamb. When He went to Calvary He became both the Lamb that was offered and the High Priest that offered the sacrifice. He is both the scapegoat of Leviticus 16 and the goat that was sacrificed. He is both the root (Creator) and offspring (Son) of David (Revelation 22:16); both the bright and morning Star and the Sun of righteousness; both the Child born and the Son given, and the mighty God and the everlasting Father (Isaiah 9:6). He is both the author and the finisher of our faith, and the First and the Last (and everything between), the Almighty (Revelation 1:8, 11).

Yes, my friend, He is everything we need, and we are complete in Him (Colossians 2:10). A person who tries to rob Him of His exalted position of being "far above all principality and power" (Ephesians 1:21) does so at his own peril, for every knee shall one day bow to Him and every tongue will "confess that Jesus Christ is Lord, to the glory of God the Father" (Philippians 2:11).

•••••••••••

Jesus Breathed on the Disciples
(John 20:22)

QUESTION:

Jesus breathed on His disciples and said, "Receive ye the Holy Ghost" (John 20:22). Does this mean that they received the Holy Ghost at this time? If so, what did they receive at Pentecost?

ANSWER:

The event of John 20:22 is a beautiful symbolism, foretaste, and promise of that which the disciples were to receive at Pentecost. Proof that they did not actually receive the filling or baptism of the Holy Ghost at that time is shown in John 7:39. The promise that they would receive the Holy Ghost was given to them, but Jesus indicated that He must first be glorified. That is, He must die, be buried, rise from the dead, ascend unto heaven, and be glorified; then He could pour out the Holy Ghost (His own Spirit) upon them.

Jesus instructed them meanwhile to tarry (wait) in the city of Jerusalem until the promise of the Father, the power from on high, the Holy Ghost, was poured out on them (Luke 24:49; Acts 1:4-5). This would certainly not have been necessary had they received the Holy Ghost at the time Jesus breathed on them in John 20:22.

That which they received at Pentecost was that which Jesus had promised them. The Apostle Peter, preaching the Pentecostal sermon, declared:

"This Jesus hath God raised up, whereof we all are witnesses. Therefore being by the right hand of God exalted, and having received of the Father the promise of the Holy Ghost, he hath shed forth this, which ye now see and hear" (Acts 2:32-33).

The Pentecostal experience was the fruit of Jesus' death, burial, resurrection, ascension, and glorification, exactly as Jesus had promised!

Undoubtedly the disciples received a blessing when Jesus breathed upon them. Probably it was a foretaste of the glorious experience of Pentecost, a "tiding-over" blessing. However, Jesus at this time had not yet ascended to receive the promise of the Father, so the disciples still lived before the benefits of Calvary were delivered to mankind. Therefore, just as our receiving the Holy Ghost is a foretaste of heaven, the earnest of our inheritance (Ephesians 1:14), so the experience the disciples received when Jesus breathed upon them was a foretaste of the Baptism of the Holy Ghost, their inheritance under the new covenant when the benefits of Calvary would finally be theirs at Pentecost.

The breathing of Jesus upon His disciples is beautifully symbolic. It symbolized the Spirit of God. Man was created a living soul by the breath of God (Genesis 2:7). Ezekiel prophesied of the still future spiritual restoration of the nation of Israel when he spoke of the dead bones being revived and restored to life by the breath of God (Ezekiel 37:9-14).

Jesus likened the birth of the Spirit to wind, or breath (John 3:8). The *Emphatic Diaglott* translates it: "The Spirit breathes where it will, and thou hearest its voice. . .

21

thus it is with every one who has been born of the Spirit." This is a powerful promise that when the Holy Ghost comes in, He will speak!

On the Day of Pentecost the Holy Ghost came with the sound of a "rushing mighty wind (literally 'hard breathing'), filling everyone in the house. And they were all filled with the Holy Ghost, and began to speak with other tongues, as the Spirit gave them utterance" (Acts 2:4). The foretaste the disciples had received in John 20:22 was now the fulness! Symbolism had been replaced by reality! The promise had become an experience!

Now comes the good news for us today. Peter declared, "For the promise is unto you [the Jews of that day], and to your children [the Jewish nation], and to all that are afar off [Gentiles, though they may be 'afar off' in both time and space—that's us!], even as many as the Lord our God shall call" (Acts 2:39). Since the promise of the Holy Ghost is to all of us today, the question of Acts 19:2 is equally for all today: "Have you received the Holy Ghost since you believed?"

••••••••••••

Preaching
to the Dead
(I Peter 3:18-19; 4:6)

QUESTION:

Please explain the meaning of I Peter 4:6 with regard to the dead. How did Jesus preach to the spirits in prison? (I Peter 3:18-19).

ANSWER:

"For this cause was the gospel preached also to them

that are dead, that they might be judged according to men in the flesh, but live according to God in the spirit" (I Peter 4:6).

This verse does not refer to the men who *were* dead, but that the gospel was preached to them that *are* dead. The meaning is that those who are now dead had the gospel preached to them while they were yet living.

The key to I Peter 3:18-19 is found in verse 20. I quote the three verses: "For Christ also hath once suffered for sins, the just for the unjust, that he might bring us to God, being put to death in the flesh, but quickened by the Spirit: By which also he went and preached unto the spirits in prison; which sometime were disobedient, when once the longsuffering of God waited in the days of Noah, while the ark was a preparing, wherein few, that is, eight souls were saved by water."

Christ went in His Spirit—the Spirit of Christ, the Spirit of God, the Holy Spirit—and preached through Noah in the days before the flood to those who now are spirits in prison. It does not mean that He went to them after they disobeyed the preaching of Noah and had died in their sins to preach to them again in prison. That false interpretation would do violence to the plain teaching of God's Word that "it is appointed unto men once to die, but after this the judgment" (Hebrews 9:27). The disobedient in Noah's day did not receive preferential treatment by having the gospel preached to them after they had died.

• • • • • • • • • • • •

Destruction of Earth and the Millennium
(II Peter 3:10)

QUESTION:

If God is going to set a kingdom up on earth, how is He going to do it if the earth has been destroyed? (II Peter 3:10). And if this is where God is going to set up a kingdom, is this where we're going to spend eternal life?

ANSWER:

The verse of Scripture to which you refer (II Peter 3:10) reads as follows:

> *"But the day of the Lord will come as a thief in the night; in the which the heavens shall pass away with a great noise, and the elements shall melt with fervent heat, the earth also and the works that are therein shall be burned up."*

The expression, "in which," refers to the close of the Day of the Lord at the end of the Kingdom Age or Millennium, when the destruction of the heavens and the earth takes place at the time of the Great White Throne Judgment (Revelation 20:11). We are plainly told that this is at the end of the thousand-year period or Millennium, and that during this time the saints will rule and reign with Christ (Revelation 20:6-7).

During this Kingdom Age, Satan shall be bound (Revelation 20:1-3), and Christ shall reign over the earth. This period is mentioned six times in Revelation 20:1-7, and is generally called the "Millennium" from the Latin words *mille* (1000) and *annum* (year), but the Scriptures call it simply the kingdom. It will be an earthly, visible kingdom, and its government will be theocratic, that is, the rule of God.

The following passages of Scripture help us to understand this truth: Matthew 25:31-34; Luke 1:30-33; Daniel 7:13-14; Revelation 19:11-15; Isaiah 24:23.

When Jesus sets up His kingdom and Satan is bound in the bottomless pit (Revelation 20:1-3), the curse will be lifted from the earth. The nature of vicious animals will revert back to the way God created them in the beginning, harmless and vegetarian (Isaiah 11:6-9). Human life will be prolonged (Isaiah 65:20-22; Zechariah 8:4). The land shall be as productive as the Garden of Eden (Amos 9:13; Isaiah 35:1; 55:13; Joel 2:24-26; 3:18).

Israel will be the head of all the nations of the earth (Deuteronomy 28:13; Isaiah 60:12), and the saints will sit with Jesus and rule the earth with Him (Matthew 19:28; Revelation 20:6).

However, this earth is not where we will spend eternity with Jesus, for at the end of the thousand years this earth will be destroyed. Then there will be new heavens and a new earth, "wherein dwelleth righteousness" (II Peter 3:13; Revelation 21:1).

But God has a special place for us, His bride. I Peter 1:4 tells us that God has begotten us unto a lively hope: "To an inheritance incorruptible, and undefiled, and that fadeth not away, reserved in heaven for you." Jesus said: "In my Father's house are many mansions: if it were not so, I would have told you. I go to prepare a place for you. And if I go and prepare a place for you, I will come again, and receive you unto myself; that where I am, there ye may be also" (John 14:2-3).

The place being prepared for us is called, the "holy city, new Jerusalem, coming down from God out of heaven, prepared as a bride adorned for her husband" (Revelation 21:2). This beautiful city is described in detail in Revelation 21:9-27, and it will be our home for all eternity. Jesus will be there, and He will be the light of the city (Revelation 21:23). We will have glorified bodies like that of Jesus after His resurrection.

> *"For our conversation is in heaven; from whence also we look for the Saviour, the Lord Jesus Christ: Who shall change our vile body, that it may be fashioned like unto his glorious body, according to the working whereby he is able even to subdue all things unto himself" (Philippians 3:20-21).*

But we are not there yet; we are still here. Our job now is to be ready for His return, and to get as many others ready for His return as possible. I am determined to make it in—how about you?

••••••••••••

Baptizing for the Dead
(I Corinthians 15:29)

QUESTION:

My sister has joined the Mormon Church, and one of the verses of Scripture they use is I Corinthians 15:29. I do not know how to explain this. I do know that it doesn't mean that we can be baptized for dead people. Would you explain it for me?

ANSWER:

I Corinthians 15:29 says, "Else what shall they do which are baptized for the dead, if the dead rise not at all? why are they then baptized for the dead?"

One thing that is sure is that there was no custom in Bible days of baptizing a living individual for one that is dead. All historians agree on this. And had there been one it is impossible to conceive of Paul mentioning it without condemning it. Such a practice would violate and contradict such verses of Scripture as Mark 16:16. Therefore that cannot be the meaning of the verse to which you refer.

Of course, Mormons do make a practice of baptizing living people for those who have died. One lady in our church was baptized over one hundred times when she was a Mormon. She told me she had been baptized over and over again in one day, each time a proxy for some other individual she had never even heard of before!

The next verse, verse 30, helps explain verse 29: "And why stand we in jeopardy every hour?" If there is to be no victorious end of the warfare in which we are engaged, why go on with it? Why continue the work of recruiting for soldiers? Individuals in God's church are dying continually and thus thinning the ranks. Why go on seeking to fill up the ranks? Why go on baptizing more converts to take the room of those who have died, if there be no resurrection? It is only because we know that there is victory at the end that we must go on with the work.

••••••••••••

Eternal Security

QUESTION:

My friend, who is a very devout member of a church, continually witnesses to me about her religion. She has shown me verses of Scripture about our security in Christ, but she says that every believer has eternal life and can never be lost. She seems to live in assurance and confidence while I am always searching my heart lest I not measure up. She says that I am unnecessarily living in fear, that God does not cast a person away because of his sin. If she is wrong, why does she seem to live a happier and more contented life than I do? I am really miserable at times.

ANSWER:

It is true that the normal Christian life of the child of God should be joyful and contented. When you received the gift of the Holy Ghost, God did not give you the spirit of fear, but of power, and of love, and of a sound mind (II Timothy 1:7). These blessings come in the Holy Ghost, and you should claim them as yours. Love, joy, and peace are fruit of the Spirit, who is in you (Galatians 5:22). And I John 4:18 tells us, "There is no fear in love; but perfect love casteth out fear: because fear hath torment."

To live a balanced Christian life, however, it is necessary to "fear" the Lord also. This is not the unclean fear or terror which is cast out by love, but a godly awe or reverence, a fear which is "the beginning of wisdom"

(Psalm 111:10). We are told to "pass the time of your so-journing here in fear" (1 Peter 1:17). Hebrews 12:28 tells us to "serve God acceptably with reverence and godly fear." It is dangerous to presume upon the grace of God, to suppose that He will ignore our sinning and save us anyhow. This can only create a false sense of security.

Your friend's assurance and confidence rest upon shaky ground indeed. Her sense of security does not proceed from the Lord or His Word, but from a false conception of what the Bible teaches. She is like the passengers on the giant steamship Titanic traveling from England to New York in April, 1912. This ship was at that time the largest ship in the world, and was so constructed that it was considered absolutely unsinkable. With complete confidence and assurance 2,223 persons booked passage aboard the Titanic without a qualm. Can you imagine the shock that shook the world when on its maiden voyage it struck an iceberg and sank in three hours with the loss of 1,517 lives? Every one of these people who tragically died believed that the ship they were on could never sink.

I do not mean to convey the thought that salvation is like a sinking ship. Far from it, the gospel ship is the "Old Ship of Zion," and it will safely reach heaven's shores. But what I am saying is that your friend's unbiblical doctrine of "eternal security" is what her trust is in, whether she will acknowledge it or not, and it is this false doctrine that is a sinking ship. An old song says:

> "Sin can never enter there,
> Sin can never enter there,
> So if at the judgment bar
> Sinful spots your soul shall mar,

You can never enter there."

To these words the Bible says, "Amen."

Permit me to point out to you some verses of Scripture to help you understand how false the teaching of unconditional eternal security is.

"For if God spared not the natural branches, take heed lest he also spare not thee. Behold therefore the goodness and severity of God: on them which fell, severity; but toward thee, goodness, if thou continue in his goodness: otherwise thou also shalt be cut off" (Romans 11:21-22).

"Christ is become of no effect unto you, whosoever of you are justified by the law; ye are fallen from grace" (Galatians 5:4).

"But exhort one another daily, while it is called Today; lest any of you be hardened through the deceitfulness of sin. For we are made partakers of Christ, if we hold the beginning of our confidence stedfast unto the end" (Hebrews 3:13-14).

(Read also II Corinthians 6:1; Galatians 4:1-11; I Thessalonians 3:5; I Corinthians 15:2-3; II Peter 2:20-22.)

One of the favorite passages used by those who advocate the "eternal security" doctrine is John 10:28: "And I give unto them eternal life; and they shall never perish, neither shall any man pluck them out of my hand." But they generally ignore verse 27, which tells us that this wonderful promise is given to His people who hear His voice and follow Him. Eternal life is ours and we are secure in Him, but there are always conditions to the promise of eternal salvation—it is never unconditional.

John H. Dearing, one of Pentecost's pioneer Bible

teachers in this century, made the following comment in the Pentecostal Bible Study Course.

"The truth concerning security in Christ is wonderful, for as long as you keep Jesus, you are just as secure as if you were already in heaven! But it is sad for men and women to rest upon a false security when there is a real one to lean upon. Yes, our eternal life is all on the condition that we receive Jesus, and keep Him in our lives.

"How some dare to ignore all the warnings in God's Word and teach contrary to Paul's instructions is hard to understand. This doctrine of eternal security has made many loose and careless in their moral life, and has caused many who once lived holy lives to say, 'No matter what I do, I can't be lost, for I have once tasted of the grace of God.' Every doctrine which is not conducive to a holy walk with God should be rejected.

"In order to believe the doctrine of 'Once in grace, always in grace,' one would have to take one of the following three stands: First, that a man filled with the Holy Ghost never could sin, and if one claiming the Holy Ghost did fall into sin, it would prove that he never was saved by grace. Another stand which a person might take would be that a saved man could backslide and go into sin, die in his sinful state, and enter heaven with the stain of sin still upon his life, and still be saved because he had once been saved. We feel sure that no one would think of taking either of these two stands.

"The only other stand that is left to take on this doctrine would be that, if a man was once saved and fell into sin, that he would be bound to get back into grace some time before he died. If we took this stand, we would be teaching that if a man backslid, as long as he lived in sin he could not die. If he wanted to live a long life, all he would have to do would be to put off getting back to God! And if he continued to sin, God would have to let him live forever in his sinful state.

"We cannot see how anyone would be willing to hold to any of these three positions, and one of them would have to be right if the doctrine were true."

In closing, may I say that the child of God who walks with God in holiness and in love, full of the Holy Ghost and obedient to His Word, does not have to fear. "The Spirit itself beareth witness with our spirit that we are the children of God" (Romans 8:16). This shows us that the Holy Ghost is essential to our salvation and true assurance. Perhaps you should start witnessing to your friend of her need of the Holy Ghost, and you can witness to her with complete confidence and full assurance.

•••••••••••

Paul's Gospel of Grace

QUESTION:

In the denominational church where I was raised, I was taught that Paul preached another gospel than the rest of the apostles preached. Since he received his gospel by revelation, we are to preach the gospel that Paul preached, which is the grace of God. According to this teaching, miracles have all ceased along with speaking in tongues. Salvation is strictly by believing on the Lord Jesus Christ, and all works such as baptism and holy living have nothing to do with salvation. Although I have been baptized in

Jesus' name and received the Holy Ghost with the evidence of speaking in other tongues, this teaching, which I received earlier, keeps coming to my mind to confuse me. Can you help me?

ANSWER:

I am well aware of the teaching to which you refer. It is put forward in an attempt to prevent people from obeying such verses of Scripture as Acts 2:38 and becoming filled with the Holy Ghost. It is an insidious doctrine because it is quite appealing to the flesh, and it allows people to sin and live worldly and still claim salvation.

However, it is a false and unscriptural teaching, and I hope that with the Lord's help you will be delivered from it as you consider the following verses of Scripture and the points made about them.

1. Paul received the gospel from the lips of Ananias, obeyed it, was baptized in Jesus' name; he also received the Holy Ghost and spoke in tongues (Acts 9:17-18; Acts 22:16; I Corinthians 14:18). This is exactly the same experience which all the apostles received.

2. Paul preached the same message to both Jew and Gentile; his message was the same that Peter preached in Acts 2:38. The one message consists of repentance, baptism in Jesus' name, and the gift of the Holy Ghost evidenced by speaking in tongues (Acts 26:19-20; Acts 13:38-39; Acts 19:1-7).

3. Miracles were performed in the ministry of Paul just as with the other apostles (Acts 14:8-10; Acts 15:12; Acts 16:16-18; Acts 19:11-12; I Corinthians 2:4; Hebrews 2:3-4).

4. The revelation Paul received (evidently while he

was in Arabia following his conversion, Galatians 1:17), he compared with the Apostle Peter upon his return (Galatians 1:18), and later with other church leaders (Galatians 2:1-2). These all agreed that Paul's message was the same as theirs, which they had received directly from the lips of the Lord Jesus Christ. They had nothing to add to the revelation which Paul had received (Galatians 2:6-9).

5. The portion of Paul's revelation that the other apostles had not previously understood fully had to do with the fact that the Gentiles could be fellow heirs with the Jewish Christians by obeying the gospel without being circumcised as were the Jews (Ephesians 3:1-7). Peter and the other apostles accepted this doctrinal position. At the first church council in Jerusalem the entire Apostolic Council agreed that Gentile Christians need not be circumcised (Acts 15). The plan of salvation that was preached by all the apostles including Paul is stated in Acts 2:38. Paul added this warning: "But though we, or an angel from heaven, preach any other gospel unto you than that which we have preached unto you, let him be accursed" (Galatians 1:8).

We can be sure Paul did not preach "any other gospel." Thank God, contrary to your former denomination's teaching, we are preaching today the very same gospel that Paul and all the other apostles preached in their day.

•••••••••••

Seventh Day Sabbath

QUESTION:
When my unsaved husband retired two years ago we

moved to a small town where there is no United Pentecostal Church. The only church that believes anything like we do is an independent Oneness church, but they observe the Saturday Sabbath. I am confused now because they make this the test of fellowship, and sometimes it seems like they are right. Yet I keep feeling something is wrong here. Our church is dead. I feel all shriveled up inside spiritually. Please help me. I am spiritually desperate and depressed.

ANSWER:

I can understand your desperation and your confusion. Being subjected to a constant bombardment of negative teachings that are themselves dead not only brings confusion into your life, but also causes your soul to shrivel. Of course, the church is dead, for its doctrine is dead; it was nailed to the cross when Jesus died.

I know the verses of Scripture that "Sabbath" keepers use (and misuse), for I was in a Saturday-keeping church myself for some time as a young man. And I know the tragic results of this teaching.

The following is taken from an article I wrote several years ago entitled "The True Sabbath." I hope it will answer your questions.

A new and better day began at Pentecost. That which was under the law was only a shadow. Pentecost brought to us the substance of that which the law foreshadowed. "The law made nothing perfect, but the bringing in of a better hope did" (Hebrews 7:19). Pentecost is the better hope!

Yet there are many today who would tell you that we are still under the law, and by that they mean the observance of a Saturday Sabbath. We must observe the letter of the law, say they, or we are under its condemnation. If this be true, modern so-called "Sabbath keepers" are themselves the worst offenders, especially in winter, for the law declares that all who have a fire in their homes on the Sabbath day were to be put to death (Exodus 35:2-3). How wonderful to know that we have been "delivered from the law" (Romans 7:6).

What law have we been delivered from? Our Sabbath-keeping friends are fond of dividing the law into two divisions, the "ceremonial law" or the ordinances, and the "moral law" or the Ten Commandments, which includes the Sabbath. Then they tell us it is not the "moral law" we are delivered from, but only the ceremonial law, the sacrifices, washings, etc.

A close look at Romans 7 informs us otherwise, however. Verse 7 tells us that the law that says "Thou shalt not covet," the moral law, the Ten Commandment law, is the law we are delivered from!

For what purpose was the law then? Simply as a "schoolmaster to bring us unto Christ" (Galatians 3:24). When we come to Christ, the law's work is finished, and "we are no longer under a schoolmaster" (verse 25). "Christ is the end of the law. . .to everyone that believeth" (Romans 10:4).

For a Christian who has been delivered from the law to return to it is to "frustrate [or render null and void] the grace of God" (Galatians 2:21). Paul asked, "How turn ye again to the weak and beggarly elements, whereunto ye desire again to be in bondage?" (Galatians 4:9). Then in verse 10 he listed the symptoms of this bondage, and foremost among them is "Ye observe days." They had gone back to "Sabbath-keeping"! Then he declared, "I am afraid of you, lest I have bestowed upon you labour in vain." To go back to Sabbath day observance is to defeat what Christ has done in your life. You have received the Holy Ghost in vain, and the labor of the minister who teaches this message is in vain.

"Remember the sabbath day to keep it holy" was the fourth commandment of the Ten Commandment law written in stones by the finger of God (Exodus 20:8; 31:18). It was written for the nation of Israel to observe in their land (no bitterly cold winters), as a shadow to point them to the light that was to come. This law is called in II Corinthians 3, the "letter that killeth" (verse 6), the "ministration of death" (verse 7), and the "ministration of condemnation" (verse 9). Whereas the New Testament salvation is called the "spirit that giveth life" (verse 6), the "ministration of the spirit" (verse 8), and the "ministration of righteousness" (verse 9). After receiving salvation through Jesus Christ, the law "written and engraven in stones" is said to be "done away" (verses 7, 11), and "abolished" (verses 13). Could anything be plainer?

Perhaps it would be objected that if the Ten Commandment law is "done away" and "abolished," there would be no commands against sins such as murder or adultery. Not so! In the first place, the bondage of the law is lifted only to those "in Christ," not for the sinner. Secondly, does there need to be a law to tell the Holy Ghost filled Christian not to murder or commit adultery? Not if there is a work done by the Holy Ghost on the inside!

Jesus said in Matthew 5:27-28, "Ye have heard that it was said by them of old time [in the Ten Commandment law], Thou shalt not commit adultery: But I say unto you, That whosoever looketh on a woman to lust after her hath committed adultery with her already in his heart." And again Jesus said, "Ye have heard that it was said by them of old time [in the Ten Commandment law], Thou shalt not kill; and whosoever shall kill shall be in danger of the judgment: But I say unto you, That whosoever is angry with his brother without a cause shall be in danger of the judgment: and whosoever shall say to his brother, Raca, shall be in danger of the council: but whosoever shall say, Thou fool, shall be in danger of hell fire" (Matthew 5:21-22).

The unregenerate man needs the force of a law and threat of severe penalty if it is broken, but the hate and lust is taken out of the heart of a man who is regenerated by the power of the Holy Ghost. No longer must a law be held over him reminding him he must not murder his brother or commit adultery with his brother's wife. The heart is changed!

Under the law a man could hate all he wanted just so he did not kill, or be consumed by lust just so he did not commit the act of adultery. Not so under grace. Here the heart is dealt with, not merely the outward actions.

Colossians 2:16-17 informs us that the law of sabbath-keeping was a "shadow of things to come." The shadow was cast backward in time to those under the law. The shadow ends when you come to the light, which is Christ. Since we have Christ, we are no longer in the shadow and have no more need of Sabbath observance.

What then was the substance which the Sabbath fore-shadowed? The Sabbath was given to Israel for a day of rest. Our rest is not in outwardly keeping a day, but our rest is in the Holy Ghost. Isaiah prophesied of this day of rest that was to come. "For with stammering lips and another tongue will he speak to this people. To whom he said, This is the rest wherewith ye may cause the weary to rest; and this is the refreshing: yet they would not hear" (Isaiah 28:11-12).

When the Holy Ghost fell at Pentecost, they spoke with tongues just as Isaiah said they would (Acts 2:1-4). They received the true sabbath of rest!

Sabbath day observance nullifies this great truth. To keep one day a week outwardly holy is to go back out of the light into the shadow. The true New Testament Sabbath keeper is the one who receives the Baptism of the Holy Ghost and lives in the Spirit. He "ceased from his own works as God did from his. Let us labour therefore to enter into that rest" (Hebrews 4:10-11).

Someone may ask, "Well, should we not set aside a day for assembling together for worship? If so, what day should it be?" Not the Old Testament seventh-day Sabbath, but a new day for a new life. It is fitting that the Lord's Day be chosen (Revelation 1:10), the day that Christ arose from the dead, and the day that the Holy Ghost was poured out, the first day of the week. Pentecost was on that day (Leviticus 23:16; Acts 2:1).

The first day of the week is not the New Testament sabbath day of rest. Our sabbath is the infilling of the Holy Ghost, which is the abiding presence of God. This makes every day a holy day of spiritual rest in Christ. The first day of the week is a day of worship, set aside to honor and worship the Lord in spirit and in truth. Only Spirit-filled believers enjoy the true sabbath today!

• • • • • • • • • • • •

Rebuking the Devil

QUESTION:

I heard a minister say that there was no place in the Bible where it tells Christians to rebuke the devil. Is this true? There is a lady in our church who is always going about rebuking the devil. If the young people do anything she dislikes she tells them they have a devil and starts rebuking the devil. Does she have this right? Is this according to the Scriptures?

ANSWER:

There is a great deal of misunderstanding today concerning the devil and what influence he has upon people.

First, there is but one devil, but many demons or evil spirits. However, for convenience sake we often say "the devil" when we really mean demons. Undoubtedly we are dealing with individual demons more than with the devil himself who is the "prince of the power of the air" (Ephesians 2:2) and the "god of this world" (II Corinthians 4:4). Always remember he is not omnipresent. Although he is in spirit-form, only God can be everywhere at the same time. Neither is he omnipotent (all-powerful) or omniscient (all-knowing). Only God has these attributes.

It is true that people can be demon possessed. But one cannot be filled with the Spirit and be demon possessed at the same time. Neither is it true that all sinners are demon possessed. They are controlled by their fallen, sinful, human natures, but not necessarily demon possessed.

It is important also to understand that there are

degrees of demon influence over an individual. One may be demon oppressed. Sickness is one form of this (Acts 10:38), as is depression, fear, nervousness, and worry, and Christians as well as sinners may be oppressed this way. But oppression is not possession. The demon power is at work on the outside to put these things upon the individual.

Then there is demon obsession. This is where the demon, although still not possessing the individual, is at work to put his thoughts into the mind and cause that person to become "obsessed" with certain tormenting, unclean, or untrue thoughts and fears. An individual, even a Christian, may sometimes accept these thoughts and become obsessed by them until he is brought under mental bondage to the demon. This could lead to demon possession.

Demon possession takes place when the demon spirit actually takes up residence in the person just as the Holy Ghost takes up residence in us when we are filled with the Spirit. Most generally an individual must wilfully give himself over to the devil for this to take place.

It is dangerous to accuse every individual who sins of having a devil or being demon possessed. Not only is it untrue, but it could lead the person to despair and fear, out of which he cannot rise. Or the individual might feel that it gives him an excuse for sinning. "I can't help it, I'm not responsible for it," he says. "The devil made me do it. If you will cast the devil out of me, then I will quit sinning." Christians oftentimes unknowingly fall into this trap and try to cast the demon out and cannot succeed because there is no demon in residence there in the first place. So the individual goes right on sinning and excusing himself for his sin, accusing the saints of not having enough power to cast the devil out.

In reality the person is responsible for his own sin. It is his own sinful fallen nature which makes him a sinner, not the devil or demons. Notice the teaching concerning this in James:

> *"But every man is tempted, when he is drawn away of his own lust, and enticed. Then when lust hath conceived, it bringeth forth sin; and sin, when it is finished, bringeth forth death" (James 1:14-15).*

It is plain that, although Satan and his demons may "tempt" and "entice," yet it is a person's "own lust" which "bringeth forth sin" in his life. It is a "cop-out" to attribute the blame to an evil spirit or demon and not to one's own fallen nature.

Now with this as a basis, let me get to your question. It seems first of all that this sister has a wrong concept of the devil and the cause of sin. If she could understand the above verse of Scripture and its application it would help here. As we said, it is extremely dangerous to tell people they have a devil.

Second, it is true we are never told in Scripture to "rebuke the devil." In Malachi 3:11 we are assured that if we pay our tithes and offerings faithfully that God will rebuke the devil for us. Jesus rebuked a demon in casting him out (Matthew 17:18), and in Jude 9 we are told that the archangel Michael dared not rail on Satan but said to him, "The Lord rebuke thee."

However, we are assured that if we will "submit ourselves to God" we can "resist the devil, and he will flee" (James 4·7). I Peter 5:9 adds that we are to resist the devil "steadfast in the faith." And we are given authority over demons and power to cast them out of people who are possessed with them (Mark 16:17). This authority comes only through the power of the name of Jesus Christ. The disciples found that the demons were "subject unto us *through thy name*" (Luke 10:17).

May I add that demons cannot be cast out of an individual that is possessed unless that person desires deliverance. If he does not want to be set free, not even the name of Jesus can dislodge the devil because God always allows an individual his choice. (See John 5:6; Matthew 15:28.)

To sum up, may I say that the lady to whom you refer is extremely foolish to accuse young people of being devil possessed because they do things they ought not. She is making them devil conscious instead of God conscious. She ought to sit down with them in a loving spirit and talk to them, carefully pointing out their sin, and endeavor to lead them to repentance (II Timothy 2:24-26; James 5:19-20).

For her to continually "rebuke the devil" causes those sinning not to accept responsibility for their own actions, and therefore not to seek God in repentance. You see, they are apt to accept the false accusation that they have a devil and are therefore not to blame for what they have done. Perhaps she should also ask God to forgive her for not having the patience and the love she should have to help these young people open their hearts to God so that they might receive forgiveness and the wonderful power of Christ in their lives.

And perhaps we all need a little more of Proverbs 4:7: "Wisdom is the principal thing; therefore, get wisdom; and with all thy getting, get understanding."

. . . .

Can a Devil Possessed Backslider Return?

QUESTION:

Can a person having once been filled with the Holy Ghost and backslidden become inhabited by a devil, and be delivered and restored?

ANSWER:

I realize the extreme sensitivity of your question from your accompanying letter. Before I answer directly, permit me to establish a scriptural foundation.

First, one can receive the Baptism of the Holy Ghost one time and one time only. An individual cannot be born spiritually twice any more than he can be born naturally twice.

When a man goes back into sin after receiving the Holy Ghost, the Spirit remains with him to strive with him, although justification, power, and blessing are gone and he is lost. He is spoiled for the world and cannot enjoy it like he did before he was saved. Therefore he goes deeper and deeper in sin, trying to bury the guilt and condemnation which the Holy Ghost is bringing upon him. Nevertheless, God faithfully continues to deal with him in love, endeavoring to woo him back by bringing the condemnation upon him.

44

Each time he sins he tramples on the blood of Jesus and is doing despite unto the Spirit of grace (Hebrews 10:29). Each time he wilfully sins (Hebrews 10:26), he pierces Christ again (the Christ nature planted within him) until finally he succeeds in crucifying Him afresh (Hebrews 6:6).

When this has finally taken place and the new nature within him has been killed, the man is reprobate (Romans 1:28). He is past feeling (Ephesians 4:19), and has become incapable of repentance (II Corinthians 7:10). His heart is given over to unbelief (Hebrews 3:12-14). He has gone through God's program and is doomed (II Thessalonians 2:10-12).

It is a horrible thing to sin after receiving the Holy Ghost!

Now to your question. At any time after his first act of disobedience and rebellion against God, it is possible for a man to give himself over to the devil to the extent he becomes demon possessed. Even then the Holy Ghost will continue to strive until he crosses the invisible line into a reprobate condition. However, when one becomes demon possessed, the devil must be cast out of him before he can be restored, for now he is not only under the power of his fleshly, carnal, rebellious nature, but also under the control of a demon power which has made him his slave. (See II Timothy 2:25-26.)

I cannot overemphasize the extreme danger that a backslider is in. He is a prey to demon power and could become possessed of the devil. But even in the event he does not become demon possessed, he is still in serious danger of crossing over into a reprobate state. These are terrible things to contemplate.

45

The question you ask, I am happy to say, can be answered in the affirmative. Yes, thank God, a person having once been filled with the Holy Ghost, who has backslidden and become devil possessed, can be delivered and restored, *if* (and we must always remember this) he genuinely wants deliverance and turns in full repentance before it is too late, and *if* he comes to God's church and ministry so that the demon may be cast out through the power of the name of Jesus Christ. This is his only hope.

Let me say in closing that as long as God's Spirit is striving it is God's assurance that He will forgive. The problem is not on God's side. He is willing and able to forgive at any time. But the problem is with the individual who persists in sinning. He may so harden his heart that he becomes incapable of repenting. But it is wonderful to know that, as dear old Brother Denny used to say, "God's all right!" (See I John 1:9.)

••••••••••••

Can a Baby Be Devil Possessed?

QUESTION:

Why are some innocent children possessed of the devil? Can a child be born already possessed by a demon or demons?

ANSWER:

All children are born with a fallen, sinful nature. A child does not have to be taught how to lie, to lose his temper, or to steal. However, a child's sin is not imputed to his account until he comes to an age when he knows right from wrong, and how to reject the one and choose the other. (See Isaiah 7:16.)

This age, often called the "age of accountability," is considered by the Roman Catholic Church to be twelve. Others place it at different ages, but I do not believe it is the same with all children. In fact, I have seen children of four or five years of age cry out to God in acknowledgement and repentance of their sins, and receive the gift of the Holy Ghost. They could not repent and turn from sin without knowing right from wrong. However, in the majority of cases it is probably between seven and ten years of age that a child becomes responsible for his sins and therefore is lost unless he obeys the plan of salvation.

If a child is born with an evil, sinful fallen nature for which he is not responsible, it is not strange that some children may be born already possessed with a demon. I have seen little infants demonstrating all the indications of being so possessed. They are tormented, ungovernable, unpredictable, given to wild rages and tantrums, manifesting abnormal vicious and destructive tendencies, both to themselves and others. It is evident that they are under the control of an evil power even in their infancy. Mark 9:21 speaks of a boy who had a demon since he was a child (Greek *paidiothen* meaning "from infancy"—Strong).

It is not beyond the realm of credibility that if a mother is possessed by several demons, one or more of them could take up residence in the child during the months she is carrying that child in her womb. However, there may also be other ways in which a child may become demon possessed besides through a demon-possessed mother. Nevertheless, pre-natal influence is a strong factor in the development of any child.

47

A mother once told me that throughout the time she was carrying her second child she was continually seeking for the Holy Ghost, then filled, and lived a life of spiritual intimacy and communion with God. All through her pregnancy she had such an experience in God that she said the only way she could describe it was to say that, like Enoch, she walked with God every day. Then she told me that this child was all its lifetime more spiritual, prayerful, easily controlled, tender, and obedient than all her other children. Early in life he dedicated himself to the service of the Lord. She felt that the exaltation she experienced during that period marked her child for its entire lifetime.

Another mother told me that the conduct of her children born before she was saved and those born after were totally different. Those born before were stubborn and disrespectful; those born after were obedient and amenable to discipline.

The spiritual, as well as physical, condition of the mother during her pregnancy apparently has a very strong bearing upon the personality of the child, both in its infancy and throughout its entire life. It is vital that those expecting children stay away from demon influences that could mark their children. This should be the most spiritual time of their lives, and the most rewarding. It will pay eternal dividends.

In closing, may I say that if you suspect that your child is troubled by demon spirits, consult your pastor. It may or may not be actual demon powers at work. If it is, do not despair. First, the child is not held responsible for that over which he had no power, that which is not of his doing. Just as a child under the "age of accountability" can lie to your face, yet not be held accountable for it, because he is not yet capable of knowing the difference between right and wrong, so an infant may be demon possessed, yet not be doomed for hell until he comes to the age of accountability where he is capable of consciously and responsibly accepting or rejecting the evil spirit.

Secondly, one of the signs Jesus promised would follow those who believe is that they would cast out demons: "In my name shall they cast out devils [demons] . . ." (Mark 16:17). Let the pastor and elders of your church lay hands on him in Jesus' name, and the evil spirits must flee. He is the same Jesus today as when He cast the demon out of the child in Mark 9:17-29. And He loves little children.

•••••••••••

Is Perfection Possible?

QUESTION:
Jesus told us to be perfect like God is perfect (Matthew 5:48). Also, Paul commanded us to be perfect (II Corinthians 13:11). Is perfection possible in this life?

ANSWER:
There are three tenses in the scriptural teaching of perfection. They are present perfection, continuing perfection, and future perfection.

Present perfection (Hebrews 10:14-17) belongs to every Christian when he is sanctified or set apart unto God by the infilling of the Holy Ghost, and can be likened to the perfection of unripe fruit. A green apple on a tree may be perfect in that it has no worms, is not diseased, shriveled, or undeveloped. It may be perfectly healthy and normal, yet be unfit to eat because it is not yet ripe.

Every normal New Testament Christian is perfect in the same sense when he receives the Holy Ghost. He has repented and been baptized in Jesus' name for the remission of his sins. His sins are under the blood, blotted out, and there is no condemnation in his life. He is perfect as an infant is perfect, but it is "green apple" perfection, and he needs to go on to maturity.

Continuing perfection is when the infant Christian begins to develop or grow into maturity. It is a process of maturation, and it should be going on in every Christian's life. We are urged not to build foundation on top of foundation, but once the foundation of the principles of the doctrine of Christ is laid in our lives to "go on unto perfection" (Hebrews 6:13). This is done by a continual cleansing both of flesh and spirit, thus "perfecting holiness in the fear of God" (II Corinthians 7:1).

This cannot be accomplished by the individual alone. Therefore God gave His church the ministry "for the perfecting of the saints" (Ephesians 4:12). The minister's task is to preach the Word to the church so that it might be "sanctified and cleansed with the washing of water by the word, that Christ might present it to Himself a glorious church, not having spot, or wrinkle, or any such thing; but that it should be holy and without blemish" (Ephesians 5:26-27).

Even though the Christian may be filled with the Holy Ghost and possess present perfection (green apple perfection), he can never be brought through a continuing

50

process of perfection to full maturity (ripe apple perfection) without the help of the ministry. How important Hebrews 13:17 is in the light of this!

Full maturity is coming to the full stature and perfection of Christ (Ephesians 4:13). This is future perfection, the goal for which we all must strive. Paul denied he had yet attained this (Philippians 3:11), yet in the same chapter, verse 15, he spoke of being perfect. This, as we have, seen was "green apple perfection" in the process of being developed into maturity.

This future perfection is nothing short of the full stature of Christ which is held up before us by both Jesus and Paul in the verses you quoted and by such other verses of Scripture as Galatians 3:3 and I Peter 1:15-16.

While we may not yet have come into the full stature and perfection of Christ, we can be "blameless" and live a life free from sin (I Corinthians 1:8; Philippians 2:15). But it is only as we "press toward the mark for the prize of the high calling of God in Christ Jesus" (Philippians 3:13) that we will be growing into maturity and be counted "blameless" and ready for the Rapture.

It is then, at the Rapture, that we will enter into the full perfection planned for us from the foundation of the world. For it is then that Christ will "change our vile bodies, that it may be fashioned like His glorious body" (Philippians 3:21).

"For this corruptible shall put on incorruption, and this mortal shall put on immortality" (I Corinthians 15:53). The great goal of all the saints of all the ages will finally have been reached, for **we shall be like him,** for we shall see him as he is" (I John 3:2).

Are Those Lost Who Never Heard?

QUESTION:

How can we say a man is lost if he has never heard the gospel? Would not God be cruel and vindictive if He condemned a man to hell simply because of our failure to get to him with the plan of salvation? I cannot think that God is so unfair.

ANSWER:

God is not cruel, vindictive, or unfair. Do not libel God in this way. For a foolish mortal to impugn God and charge Him, even by implication as you have, with base designs on the human beings He so lovingly created in His image, is an unspeakable insult. You must not lend your mind to Satan to entertain such thoughts, which will surely lead you into terrible darkness and despair.

You are ignorant of some very basic truths of the Word of God. You must believe God's Word that God is a kind, loving, merciful heavenly Father, grieved over man's sin, who is not willing to leave a stone unturned to save and rescue him from hell.

Let me give you some very important foundational verses of Scripture to help you.

> *"The Lord is. . .not willing that any should perish, but that all should come to repentance" (II Peter 3:9).*
>
> *"God. . .is the Saviour of all men, specially of those that believe" (I Timothy 4:10).*
>
> *"For God so loved the world, that he gave his only begotten Son, that whosoever believeth in him*

*should not perish, but have everlasting life. For
God sent not his Son into the world to condemn
the world; but that the world through him might
be saved" (John 3:16-17).*

It is not God who condemns men to hell. He is the
Savior. His purpose is to save, not condemn. John 3 continues: "He that believeth on him is not condemned: but
he that believeth not is condemned already, because he
hath not believed in the name of the only begotten Son
of God. And this is the condemnation, that light is come
into the world, and men loved darkness rather than light,
because their deeds were evil" (verses 18-19).

Hell and the lake of fire were not made for man, but
for Satan and his angels (Matthew 25:41). Satan took the
human race captive while the race was still in the loins
of Adam and Eve. When he beguiled Eve (II Corinthians
11:3), and Adam deliberately disobeyed (Romans 5:19),
the entire human race was plunged into sin.

*"Wherefore, as by one man sin entered into
the world, and death by sin; and so death passed
upon all men, for that all have sinned" (Romans
5:12).*
*"For as in Adam all die. . ." (I Corinthians
15:22).*

But God was not willing for Satan to have the human
race, even though mankind deliberately chose to turn their
backs on God and serve the devil.

"Therefore as by the offence of one judgment

53

> *came upon all men to condemnation; even so by*
> *the righteousness of one the free gift came upon*
> *all men unto justification of life" (Romans 5:18).*
>   *"For the wages of sin is death; but the gift of*
> *God is eternal life through Jesus Christ our Lord"*
> *(Romans 6:23).*

Never forget that we "all have sinned and come short of the glory of God" (Romans 3:23). We were "all as an unclean thing" (Isaiah 64:6). We all deserved hell, and "were by nature the children of wrath" (Ephesians 2:3). It is important that we understand that every man is a sinner, lost, corrupt, depraved in his natural state, and a slave to Satan. Ephesians 2 tells the story.

> *"You. . .were dead in trespasses and sins:*
> *Wherein in time past ye walked according to the*
> *course of this world, according to the prince of the*
> *power of the air, the spirit that now worketh in*
> *the childen of disobedience: Among whom also we*
> *all had our conversation [manner of life] in times*
> *past in the lusts of our flesh, fulfilling the desires*
> *of the flesh and of the mind; and were by nature*
> *the children of wrath, even as others" (verses 1-3).*

What a bleak and hopeless picture! Verse 12 adds that "at that time ye were without Christ, being aliens from the commonwealth of Israel, and strangers from the covenants of promise, having no hope, and without God in the world." But God, who is love (I John 4:8), was not willing for mankind to be lost and without hope. He plannned salvation for mankind! And so we are told:

"But God, who is rich in morcy, for his great love wherewith he loved us, even when we were dead in sins, hath quickened us together with Christ (by grace ye are saved)" (Ephesians 2:4-5).

"But now in Christ Jesus ye who sometimes were far off are made nigh by the blood of Christ" (Ephesians 2:13).

The poet tells the story beautifully:

"There was One who was willing to die in my stead
That a soul so unworthy might live;
And the path to the cross He was willing to tread
All the sins of my life to forgive.
They are nailed to the cross,
*   they are nailed to the cross;*
Oh, how much He was willing to bear.
With what anguish and loss Jesus went to the cross
And He carried my sins with Him there."

Does this sound like a God who is anxious to plunge sinners into hell? Never! If a man goes to hell it will be because he deserves to go there.

But the question is asked, "How about the one who never heard? Will he go to hell because he never had a chance?"

It is my firm conviction that if a man hungers and thirsts after righteousness he shall be filled (Matthew 5:6), no matter who he is, or what measure of the gospel story he has heard up to that point. Let me explain. A measure of light is given to every man at some particular point in his life (John 1:9). If a man is a good and just man who hungers and thirsts after righteousness, and he walks in that measure of light, more light will be given to him. Proverbs 4:18 says that "the path of the just is as the shining light, that shineth more and more unto the perfect day." If he does not walk in that light there need be no more brought to him, for he would not walk in it if it were brought (II Corinthians 4:3-4). But if he walks in the small measure of light given him, God is duty bound by His righteousness to bring greater light to him.

> *"God is light, and in him is no darkness at all. If we say that we have fellowship with him, and walk in darkness, we lie, and do not the truth: But if we walk in the light, as he is in the light, we have fellowship one with another, and the blood of Jesus Christ his Son cleanseth us from all sin"* (I John 1:5-7).

Cornelius is a striking example of this. He was "a devout man, and one that feared God with all his house, which gave much alms to the people, and prayed to God alway" (Acts 10:2), yet he was unsaved (Acts 11:14). But as he walked in the measure of light he possessed, his acts of devotion to God and man went up for a memorial (Acts 10:4), and moved God to move upon one of His preachers to bring to Cornelius the message of salvation and the opportunity to walk in that greater light. God did this even though it meant a drastic and revolutionary change in the minds and attitudes of Christians who had refused to share the gospel with others. As a result Cornelius received the full light of the gospel and was saved.

This shows us how important it is for God's church

to get the gospel out to the world. Paul knew himself to be a debtor to the world because he had the gospel of salvation, and the world had never heard it (Romans 1:14-16; 10:13-15). We owe the world the gospel of salvation today!

Friend, how dare you accuse God of being unfair, even by implication? He will see to it that every man has full opportunity to walk in light. Whether he receives the full light or not depends upon whether he walks in the measure of light he does possess.

I hope *you* will walk in the light of the truth of the Word *you* have received, and never again even breathe the devil's dark lie that God sends men to hell because they never had a chance when actually the very opposite is true. "He is not willing that any should perish, but that all should come to repentance." How wonderful God is!

●●●●●●●●●●●●

Life On Other Planets

QUESTION:

I have heard that the Bible describes flying saucers in the Scriptures, such as II Kings 2:11 and Ezekiel 1:4-28. Is this true? Does God acknowledge flying saucers or existence of life on other planets?

ANSWER:

Of course, there is life in the universe besides on our planet; if not, where do the angels live? There are many, many spirit beings. Angels are said to be innumerable (Hebrews 12:22), but we know there are more than 104 million (10,000 X 10,000 + 2,000 X 2,000—Revelation 5:11). The devil probably has at least one-half that many fallen angels under his control (Revelation 12:4).

Angels are created beings, and while they do not multiply (Matthew 22:30), they have access to the heavenlies and the throne of God (Job 1:6; Matthew 18:10). This means that they undoubtedly traverse the solar system and the universe, but I am sure they do not use flying saucers to do so.

Human life or life such as ours is another thing, however. I do not believe there is such life on any other place in the universe than on this earth. If there were other places inhabited by men, Jesus would have to die on each one, or else they would be sinless creatures, for He made the universe and everything in it.

II Kings 2:11 and Ezekiel 1:4-28 do not describe flying saucers.

•••••••••••

Capital Punishment

QUESTION:
Is capital punishment scriptural?

ANSWER:
Since the creation, God has dealt with man through seven great covenants. There are, in order: the Adamic Covenant, Noahic, Abrahamic, Mosaic, Hebraic, Davidic, and the New Covenant.

Some of these were superceded by a later covenant, such as the Mosaic, which has been displaced by the New

Covenant. But most of them are covenants which, when once established, continue on throughout the life of man on earth. An example is the Adamic Covenant, in which Satan was cursed, multiplied sorrow was visited upon womanhood, the earth was cursed, and man was consigned to wearisome toil. Sorrow of life became man's common lot, and physical death became inevitable. All of these provisions are still in effect today.

Another covenant in which the conditions are perpetual and still in effect is the Noahic Covenant wherein God authorized the institution of human government. Here God gave man the right to set up governmental procedures and laws, and punish violators. One of the principles which God laid down by which human government was to operate involved capital punishment: "Whoso sheddeth man's blood, by man shall his blood be shed" (Genesis 9:6).

It must always be kept in mind that God never contradicted or nullified this principle. Later, when God instituted the Mosaic Covenant in which the Ten Commandments were the foundation, He included "Thou shalt not kill" (Exodus 20:13). Literally this means, "Thou shalt do no murder," and if one were to slay another, the punishment would revert back to God's principle established under the Noahic Covenant, and capital punishment would be inflicted. (See Exodus 21:12-14; Numbers 35:30; Deuteronomy 17:6.)

Thus we see that God is the author of capital punishment; that when He authorized man to set up rules of conduct and penalties for violating those rules He specifically insisted that capital punishment be included.

In conclusion, may I say that God's purpose was that man would be responsible to govern the world for God.

How sad it is to find out that instead of man governing for God he has governed the world for himself. This is apparent on every side, and the result is tragic indeed.

•••••••••••

Are the Wicked in Hell Now?

QUESTION:

If the dead are already in hell burning, will they come out of hell to be judged? Is the Rich Man (Luke 16:19-31) in hell now? I can't see how and why they would have to come out of hell to be judged if they are already in hell burning.

ANSWER:

It is important that we understand properly the story Jesus gave us of the Rich Man and Lazarus recorded in Luke 16:19-31. Many who do not wish to accept this as a true account claim that it is only a parable and therefore cannot be counted upon as a trustworthy and true account of what happens after death.

However, I strongly believe it to be a true and factual account of two men who lived and died, and that probably Jesus knew them both during His sojourn here on earth. In fact, Jesus Himself indicated that the story was true when He started the story with "There was a certain rich man." (Contrast this with the many places where it reads, "And he spake this parable unto them.") Further evidence is seen in the fact that Jesus identified the one who was saved by name, calling him Lazarus, and placed him with Abraham, who was certainly a real

60

person.

Even though I firmly believe the story of the Rich Man and Lazarus truly occurred and that these were actual men, still it is not necessary to believe this to know that the story is factual. Even if it were a parable, it would not mean that the events in it are not to be believed, for Jesus never told a parable which was not true-to-life in every detail. Why would He concoct a story that on the face of it was not to be believed? Every parable Jesus told was of a event that could have happened just as He told it.

So we may assuredly believe the story of the Rich Man and Lazarus to be absolutely true to fact, and the events described to be exactly as they actually happened. The major difference between the story and the way things are now is that Paradise (which in Luke 16 Jesus called by the name of "Abraham's bosom," the title the Jews themselves used to describe it) was removed from its former place across the great gulf from hell (or *hades*) up to the very throne of God by Jesus when He ascended. (See Psalm 63:18; Ephesians 4:8; II Corinthians 12:1-4). Now when a child of God dies, his soul is immediately at rest in the heavenlies in the presence of God. (See Philippians 1:23; II Corinthians 5:8.) When Jesus comes again He will bring the souls of those who sleep in Jesus back with Him (I Thessalonians 4:14) to be reunited with their glorified bodies rising from the grave.

Now we will try to answer your question. First, notice that the Rich Man was in the torments of hades while his brothers still lived on earth (Luke 16:27-28). Undoubtedly he is still there, awaiting the Great White Throne Judgment (Revelation 20:11-15).

In Revelation 20:13, we see that the earth and the

sea shall give up the bodies of the wicked dead, the word *death* referring to the grave. At the same time hell *(hades)* will give up what is there, that is, the souls of the wicked dead, and the bodies and souls are reunited. This is the "second resurrection." These shall then all stand before God, who shall judge them out of those things written in the books, according to their works (Revelation 20:12).

Then, after they are judged and their doom pronounced against them, all the wicked shall be cast, both soul and body, into the lake of fire, which is the second death (Revelation 20:14).

Only the souls of the wicked are in torment in hades now while the body is in the grave. Then, at the "second resurrection," one thousand years after the "first resurrection" and the Rapture of the church, the bodies and souls of the wicked shall be reunited to be judged and cast into the lake of fire, which will be their doom for all eternity.

You may wonder why it is done this way. Well, a man who is apprehended in the commission of a crime will be thrown into jail immediately. However, later he is brought before a judge, tried and convicted for his crime, and sentenced to prison where he will spend his life carrying out the sentence meted to him by the judge.

So the soul of a wicked man upon dying will go immediately to hades (the jailhouse), awaiting the judgment (Hebrews 9:27), to hear the sentence of doom pronounced upon him. Then he will be cast into the lake of fire (prison) to serve the terrible sentence of the lost in that awful place. The judgment is necessary so "that every mouth may be stopped, and all the world became guilty before God" (Romans 3:19).

2

Christian Living

Suing at Law
(Matthew 5:40)

QUESTION:

Would you please explain Matthew 5:40: "And if any man will sue thee at the law, and take away thy coat, let him have thy cloak also."

ANSWER:

It is wrong to go to law with your Christian brother (I Corinthians 6:1-8). Verse 7 tells us that it would be better to suffer wrong than to go to the law in a complaint against another Christian. God's Word gives us procedures to follow when a brother in the church wrongs us (Matthew 18:15-17). The settlement should be made within the confines of the church and not before the ungodly.

The verse of Scripture to which you refer, however, is not necessarily dealing with a Christian going to law with another Christian. This is a case where a sinner goes to law against a Christian and obtains judgment against him. The sinner is awarded the Christian's coat. Evidently the court determined that the Christian was at fault. It may be that the Christian felt he was innocent of any wrongdoing, or that he did it unwittingly and without intention; nevertheless, it is evident that he did defraud the sinner, at least to the satisfaction of the court. This put the Christian in a very bad light. The verdict of the court was that he defrauded the sinner, and that he must pay for it with his coat.

The purpose of the law is to bring about equity. The Christian should never have to be forced by the law to do the right thing—he should make things right without having to be compelled by the law to do so. Actually, the law is not for the Christian; he should not need the law to compel him to be just and honorable.

> *"But we know that the law is good, if a man use it lawfully; knowing this, that the law is not made for the righteous man, but for the lawless and disobedient, for the ungodly and for sinners, for unholy and profane, for murderers of fathers and murderers of mothers, for manslayers, for whoremongers, for them that defile themselves with mankind, for liars, for perjured persons, and if there be any other thing that is contrary to sound doctrine" (I Timothy 1:8-10).*

If a man is a sinner and a lawbreaker, the church cannot judge him for he is not subject to the church; he needs a policeman and a court of law to deal with him. It is necessary sometimes for Christians to call the law on lawbreakers, for "the law is for the lawless."

In closing, may I say that it is a shame for a Christian to be judged guilty of defrauding another man. If this should occur, the Christian should show sorrow for his lapse of godly behavior by not only taking his punishment and making restitution, but he should do more. He should go beyond the law's requirements of surrendering his coat, and "let him have his cloak also."

I am sure if more Christians carried out the wonderful teachings of Jesus in the "Sermon on the Mount," it would result in bringing untold multitudes to their knees as they behold the beautiful Christlike spirit manifested by those who claim to be the followers of the lowly Nazarene.

．．．．．．．．．．．．

Telling the Church
(Matthew 18:17)

QUESTION:

When it says "tell it [that is, the trespass of your brother] unto the church" in Matthew 18:17, does it mean to tell the matter to the congregation of the church?

ANSWER:

The context of the verse of Scripture reveals God's way of dealing with problems arising between individuals in the church. (See verses 15-16.) If this plan would be strictly adhered to, it would solve many problems before they get so big that they cause trouble in the church. Saints should be mature enough to go to one another in the right spirit to work out their differences without having to involve the pastor until it is necessary.

If the one who has been wronged goes to the other as this verse of Scripture teaches, but the other will not listen to him, the wronged one should then go to the pastor for advice. He should ask advice as to whom he should take with him when he goes the second time to the offender. Quite often the offending person will be willing to clear up the difficulty during this second step, especially if he knows that the third step will be taken if he does not.

The third step brings us to your question. If the offending one does not make things right when he has been approached by the injured person alone, or when the aggrieved individual has brought one or two others with him, then it is time for the offended one to "tell it to the church." Just who is it to whom he should tell it?

I do not believe this verse means for the injured brother to rise up in a public service to relate how he was wronged and to accuse his brother. Neither do I believe that there should be an open trial of the matter before the saints. Churches have been torn up, saints have been injured, congregations have polarized into two camps, accusations have been hurled, new converts have stumbled, tempers have flared, gossipers have had a field day, and carnality has reigned supreme by such unwise methods based upon a false understanding of this verse.

God's church is composed of two parts, which together function as "the church": the saints and the ministry. God has placed the ministry in charge as "overseers" (Acts 20:28). They have the responsibility to "reprove, rebuke, exhort" (II Timothy 4:2). They are the ones God has placed in the church to discipline. And these are the ones in the church to adjudicate matters between saints.

The third step, therefore, is when the pastor, representing the entire church, takes a hand in the matter. It is turned over into his hands and he hears the testimony of the aggrieved one, plus those who went with him the second time.

Then the pastor is obligated to take action. He endeavors to bring the persons together, to get the offender to do the right thing. If a person won't listen to his pastor, he is in deep trouble! God stands behind His ministry, and it is a very serious matter to lie to him, or to dishonor him, or to disobey him.

The story of Ananias and Sapphira ought to teach us

something. (See Acts 5:1-11.) We had better listen to and obey God's minister for a person cannot go over his head!

If the one who has wronged the other still will not repent and straighten out his trespass after being dealt with by the pastor, it then turns into the most serious of all matters. This is where God stands behind the actions of His church, and this man is to be considered no longer as a brother, but henceforth as a heathen man or a sinner.

If more Christians would use this scriptural way of solving difficulties, to start by approaching the offender personally and privately in the right spirit, I am convinced there would be far less trouble in our churches. Too many try to by-pass God's order. They want the pastor to take the first step. This is not God's way. It is each person's job to go to the other individual first, in an endeavor to work the problem out, between the two of them.

Most big problems start out as little ones that never get properly resolved. These become running sores that eventually add up and become feuds, causing the pastor much needless heartache and frustration. Do it God's way! It works!

•••••••••••

Two or Three Witnesses
(II Corinthians 13:1)

QUESTION:

II Corinthians 13:1 says that "In the mouth of two or three witnesses shall every word be established." Does this mean that we must have at least two or three verses of Scripture on any subject before we believe it?

ANSWER:

If you take the Old Testament Scriptures from which Paul is quoting in II Corinthians, you will find that the context refers to a man accused of a crime. He cannot be judged guilty at the mouth of only one witness. There must be at least two witnesses accusing him before a judgment of guilty can be rendered and punishment meted out. (See Deuteronomy 17:6; 19:15.) The Old Testament passages do not refer to any requirement that a certain truth must be mentioned two or three times in the Scriptures before it is to be accepted.

And Paul, in the verse referred to, is not implying that two or more verses are needed to establish a truth. The context indicates that Paul is concerned about the carnal condition of the Corinthian church. He tells them in the first part of the verse, "This is the third time I am coming to you." Then he says, "In the mouth of two or three witnesses shall every word be established."

In verse two he enumerates the three witnesses: the first witness is his warning to them on a previous visit about their carnality; the second witness is the letter he was writing to them, again warning them; and the third witness will occur when he visits them. If he finds them unrepentant, he forewarned them, "I will not spare." Thus he used the quotation from the Old Testament in the same sense it was originally intended—that of accusing, proving guilt, and meting out punishment.

Let us remember that "All Scripture is given by inspiration of God" (II Timothy 3:16). Therefore if one verse teaches something plainly, it is as much settled and certain as though it were restated in a dozen places. We do not need two or three scriptural references to believe a

Bible truth that is plainly stated in one verse of Scripture.

It is only when someone places an interpretation upon the meaning of a verse that corroborating verses of Scripture are needed to prove the truth of that interpretation. This is something vastly different from needing two or three verses of Scripture on a subject before believing what the Bible has to say.

An example of this is Matthew 28:19. Oneness people believe this verse strongly just as it is written. It is only when trinitarians attempt to interpret the verse to mean that Jesus set forth the formula of words to repeat at baptism that Oneness believers say, "Whoa! Show me corroborating Scriptures that support your interpretation." Of course, there are none. It is only the interpretation that needs corroborating Scriptures before it is to be believed, not Matthew 28:19 itself.

In this connection, a safe rule to follow concerning whether any verse is correctly interpreted or not relating to the doctrine of the Early Church is: first, the plain statement of Scripture setting it forth; and second, the practice or custom of the church of that day as declared in the New Testament. A few examples of this procedure are:

Baptism in the name of Jesus. *Statement:* Acts 2:38-39; *practice* Acts 8:16; 10:48; 19:5.

Tongues, the initial evidence of the Baptism of the Holy Ghost. *Statement:* Isaiah 28:11-12; *practice:* Acts 2:4; 10:45-46; 19:6.

Uncut hair for women, short hair for men. *Statement:* I Corinthians 11:4-15; *practice* I Corinthians 11:16 (literally we do not practice any other custom than this, neither do the churches of God).

Literal communion. *Statement:* I Corinthians 11:23-34; *practice* Acts 2:42.

●●●●●●●●●●●●

Public or Private Confession
(James 5:16)

QUESTION:

In James 5:16 it says, "Confess your faults one to another, and pray one for another that ye may be healed." Does this mean to tell our faults to saints in the church?

ANSWER:

I am aware that the word *faults* (Greek *paraptoma*) in this verse of Scripture is translated "sins" in some translations. But I am convinced that the root meaning of *paraptoma* is different from the ordinary one for "sin" (Greek *hamartia*), which means "failing to hit the mark, a sin, whether by omission or commission in thought, word, or deed" (Bullinger). (See *The Companion Bible*, appendix, page 161.) *Paraptoma* is more nearly approximated by the word *fault* than *sin*, and may be understood to mean the weakness of character which caused one to commit the sin.

Some years ago I purchased a teapot for my wife. The very first time she used it, it broke. When I examined the pieces I discovered a hidden flaw in the porcelain of the pot which gave way when the hot liquid was poured into it. The flaw we might liken to the fault *(paraptoma)*, resulting in the tea being spilled, which we could call the sin *(hamartia)*.

Now let us apply this to the verse in question. I certainly believe this verse means to confess to other Christians one's faults. But if a man has been beating his wife, it would bring shame and disgrace upon the church for the man to get up in a public service and confess, "Saints, pray for me that I might quit beating my wife." If he does this, he is confessing the sin *(hamartia)* and not the fault *(paraptoma)* or flaw in his character that caused him to commit the sin.

How more scriptural it would be for him to say, "Saints, pray for me that I might get victory over my terrible temper." His ungovernable temper was the fault *(paraptoma)* and that caused him to commit the sin *(hamartia)* of beating his wife. It is not easy for an individual to confess he has a weakness. It is easier for him to just acknowledge the deed but cover the fault by intimating that the fault was the other individual's who provoked him.

In confessing his fault, a person gets at the root cause of his sin, acknowledging that the fault was his, and doing it in such a way as not to bring disgrace upon God's church. How much better it is to get the victory over the cause than to merely quit the sin and have it break out in another way, perhaps even worse because the fault was never dealt with!

How then should we confess sins? First, they should always be confessed to God. Then it is sometimes good to go to the pastor and confess our sins. A secret is always safe with a true man of God, for he would never breathe it to a soul. But to confess secret sins to others indiscriminately is unwise and unnecessary.

A good rule to follow is this: A confession should be

just as broad as the offense. If the sin was secret it should be confessed secretly; if it was done against an individual, it should be confessed to that individual; if it was committed openly or if it is generally known, it should be confessed openly.

But always remember, only the blood of Jesus can cleanse sin. When we come to Calvary in confession and full repentance, we graciously receive the promise, "If we confess our sins he is faithful and just to forgive us our sins and to cleanse us from all unrighteousness" (I John 1:9).

••••••••••••

Widow Plays Tennis With a Married Man

QUESTION:

I am a widow and still in my 30's. I am a friendly person, outgoing, and like to have friends and a good time, but I am not looking for a husband. I don't know exactly what to do about friends. When you have been married, you don't pick friends with the unmarried as they are too young, so your friends are among the young married couples around your age. I have been criticized for being friendly with a certain young couple. I like sports and play tennis with the husband of the couple. I have no desire for this man and it is all good, clean fun. The wife doesn't mind at all. She knows her husband loves her and that there is nothing whatsoever between us. Do you think this is wrong, or is it just some evil minded people hatching something up?

74

ANSWER:

I do not know about the evil minded people hatching something up. But I do know that pure minded people, people who have the mind of Christ, are exceedingly careful not to give occasion to the flesh, and to avoid the very appearance of evil.

These are days when anything goes, and people do not see any wrong in it. There is a continuous, subtle, brainwashing process going on among God's people, especially among those who are not really deeply spiritual. May I ask you, how much praying do you do? How much fasting? How much Bible reading do you do every day? Are you involved in witnessing, Sunday school teaching, or in teaching home Bible studies? If not, why not? Apparently you have time for other things, why not spiritual things?

You are off base to have "fun" and play tennis with the man, especially if his wife is not with you. If she does not come with you, then politely decline his invitation to play tennis the next time the man invites you. If you need the exercise, I am sure there are some other sisters in the church who would play tennis with you. By the way, what kind of dresses do you wear when you are out playing tennis with someone else's husband?

If you cannot see what is wrong with this type of arrangement, then you need to let the Holy Ghost teach you. I think that if you were really a genuine Christian and not a phony, you would find your companionship elsewhere, and not with a married man.

•••••••••••

Receiving Guidance From a Friend

QUESTION:

Recently a person very dear to me said, "The Lord showed me vividly in a dream there is something lacking in your spiritual make up. You had better correct it." I did what this person told me to do. Why didn't the Lord show my pastor what I needed? I have had the Holy Ghost for quite some time.

ANSWER:

Although you may have had the Holy Ghost for quite some time as you say, it is apparent that you are spiritually immature. Instead of blaming your pastor for not dealing with you, you need to "examine yourself" (II Corinthians 13:5). That is your task, not the preacher's.

It is also apparent that you lean spiritually upon this other individual, perhaps more than you should. And it could very well be that what faults you had that you thought were hidden were obvious to one close enough to be your "very dear" friend. Whether the "dream" was from the Lord or not, at least the warning you received stirred you.

However, do not depend upon someone else's dreams or warnings to keep you in line. That is the earmark of a foolish virgin ("Give us of your oil"). You need to maintain such a prayer life and consecration that you have an experience with God of such depth and consistency that you never again will need someone else to get you back in harmony with God.

And may I say in closing that your friend should never

76

feel that he can take the pastor's place in dealing with the saints. Some people get the idea that since God used them once in a certain way that that is now their ministry. Your friend should never assume that it is now his ministry or place to set others right in the church. He should always go to the pastor with his "dreams" before he tries to use them as a basis for correcting others.

•••••••••••

Conduct in Restaurants

QUESTION:
The Bible says, "Judge not that ye be not judged." But how can I keep from judging? To explain, I habituate a certain eating place where many of the saints come, and I am on good terms with the waitresses. They tell me that certain ones from our church are extremely critical, talk loudly about the pastor and other saints, make unreasonble or impossible demands about the food, leave little or no tip, make insulting remarks, and have even walked out without paying. I am ashamed and embarrassed, for I have witnessed to these young ladies and invited them to church until they told me these things. What should I do, and how can I keep the right attitude toward these church members, especially in view of the scriptural teaching not to judge?

ANSWER:
The Scripture verse you quote (Matthew 7:1) is a warning against attributing wrong motives, for we cannot see the heart of an individual. But Jesus, in speaking of people's actions, informed us in the same chapter, verse

16, "Ye shall know them by their fruits." Someone has wisely said, "We are not judges, but we are fruit inspectors!" Well put!

So while we are not to judge the motives of people, we certainly should not condone ungodly and unchristian actions. Wrong is always wrong when it is condemned by the Scriptures, and it is not judging to say so!

I am sorry that some "saints" act like "aints." We need to realize how our foolish and carnal actions have far-reaching effects in the lives of others. How tragic it is that often the careless talk and actions of a few church members destroy the good all the others may endeavor to do. Probably the waitresses of this particular restaurant will never come to the church and be saved, even though they have been witnessed to. Sadly enough, this is not an isolated instance.

I have often seen how saints will go out after service to some popular eating spot and "let down their hair." Loud, boisterous talk and horseplay will take place, and sometimes it degenerates into actual disgraceful conduct.

Very early in my Christian life I was taught to watch out for a let-down after a full day of services. Even good saints get weary after devil-fighting all day, and they can easily get overly silly, or overly touchy. It is at this point that Satan can take advantage of us. Innocent fellowship can degenerate into a party and become downright carnal and foolish. Oftentimes in a restaurant with the saints around we forget that the waiters and waitresses are spectators to all that we do and say. Thoughtless and careless conduct can bring dishonor to God and His cause.

Let us always remember we are Christians, in a restaurant as well as at church. Bad manners, uncouth remarks, discourtesy of any kind should never be resorted to by Bible Christians. Waitresses are not slaves—they should be treated with respect and consideration. You are put on display by God to be His representative. Always conduct yourself in such a way that your testimony will be received, and Jesus Himself will be pleased.

I have never forgotten a sampler that my godly grandmother had on the wall of her little cottage:

"Christ is the head of this home,

The unseen Guest at every meal,

And the silent Listener to every conversation."

I do not think we should ever forget that the last two lines are as true in a restaurant as they are at home.

Every saint needs to learn to guard his words and actions so that he might be pleasing to God. Then we will most assuredly find ourselves judging, not others, but as God's Word declares we must: "If we would judge ourselves, we should not be judged" (I Corinthians 11:31).

....

What Should Be our Priorities?

QUESTION:

What should come first in serving the Lord God, church, or family? And in what order?

ANSWER:

Of course, God should always be first. If He comes first you will find that His directions for the other two, church and family, do not conflict. That is, His Word instructs us to both love and care for our families and also to reach out through church activities to meet the needs of others.

When we obey such verses of Scripture as I Timothy 5:8 and Ephesians 5:21-25, which have to do with our responsibility toward the members of our family, we are actively serving God just as much as when we are knocking on doors inviting people to Sunday school, only in a different way.

May I add that many a young man with God's call on his life has ruined himself so far as the ministry is concerned because he has not diligently maintained the proper relationship with his wife and family. God considers our home life to be of paramount importance, and if one does not take time to care for his own family and maintain a proper relationship, he jeopardizes his place in God's church and program. (See I Timothy 3:2-5, 11-12; Titus 1:6.)

This principle applies not only to the ministry, but to all who serve the Lord in some capacity.

I advocate that each week, one night should be reserved for the husband and wife to spend together, perhaps eating out, just enjoying each other's presence and companionship. Wives and children need the attention of the man of the house. This is doing God's will just as much as is preaching or witnessing.

Someone has aptly said, "What shall it profit a man if he should gain the whole world and lose his family?"

• • • • • • • • • • • •

Convincing Others of the Truth

QUESTION:
My brother once studied for the ministry in the Assemblies of God. How can I convince him that "Jesus Name" is the right way? I've only been in the Lord six months.

ANSWER:
Your job is to plant the seed, not to "convince" your brother. You probably cannot match your brother in knowledge of the Word. But you have both the Spirit and the truth. After you have simply witnessed to your brother of the truth of baptism in Jesus' name, you have done your part. Then you must depend upon the Holy Ghost to finish the work and convict and draw your brother into the truth.

You did not say, but presumably your brother has received the Baptism of the Holy Ghost. If that is so, then depend upon John 16:13: "Howbeit, when he, the Spirit of truth, is come, he will guide you into all truth." This means that God's Spirit in your brother will take your witness and use it together with His Word and lead him into the truth of which you have testified.

Live a radiant, happy, victorious Christian life before your brother. He cannot help but be drawn, as the Spirit of God works in his life.

He may become argumentative, but do not argue with him. His argumentative spirit may be a sign that he is not as sure as he once was, but he may not yet be willing to surrender. This may be the time to call your pastor to talk with him. When your brother sees you will not argue but are calm and assured in your spirit of the rightness of baptism in the name of Jesus Christ, it will affect him even more.

And then pray! "The effectual fervent prayer of a righteous man availeth much" (James 5:16). Use sugar and salt: a sweet spirit and travailing prayer. What a combination! Then watch God work.

•••••••••••

"Why Did My Little Girl Die?"

QUESTION:

My little girl was killed in an accident. I know she was saved, but where is she? Is she just asleep? Also, why did she have to die? I miss her so much. Why would the Lord take her and leave my other two daughters who are not saved? They deserved to die more than she did.

ANSWER:

I can understand and sympathize with your deep sorrow. But there is One who can comfort you far better than I, One who is "touched with the feeling of our infirmities," for He was "in all points tempted like as we are, yet without sin" (Hebrews 4:15). The next verse tells us that we then can "come boldly unto the throne of grace, that we may obtain mercy, and find grace to help in time of need." How wonderful!

I think much of your sorrow results from your perplexity and lack of understanding of some very wonder-

ful scriptural truths. Permit me to give you a very brief
outline to help you here.

Man is a tripartite being, composed of spirit, soul, and
body (I Thessalonians 5:23). When an individual dies, his
spirit returns to God who gave it (Ecclesiastes 12:7), and
the body is put into the ground to return to dust. But the
soul, the real person, goes either to paradise or to hell,
depending upon whether he is saved or not. The soul remains conscious after death (Revelation 6:9-11).

The story of Lazarus and the rich man that Jesus re-
lated in Luke 16 graphically illustrates this. Let us realize
first that this is a true story, not a parable. The parables
of Jesus are almost invariably prefaced in Luke by words
such as, "He spake a parable unto them, saying. . . ." But
Jesus opened this story by plainly telling us He is *not*
relating a parable. He said, "There was a certain rich
man" and "there was a certain beggar named Lazarus"
(Luke 16:19-20).

Jesus said that the beggar died (verse 22). Probably
his body was buried in the potter's field, but Jesus said
that he "was carried by the angels into Abraham's bosom," the Jewish expression for Paradise. It was not his
body that was carried into Paradise, but it was that portion of him that lived after death, his soul.

Then Jesus said that "the rich man also died and was
buried." That is, his body was buried. But verse 23 says,
"in hell he lift up his eyes, being in torments." Since the
rich man was not saved, his soul went immediately into
the torments of hell. He was conscious in hell, just as
Lazarus was conscious in Paradise.

As Jesus continued to unfold the story, we discover
that the rich man possessed certain qualities just as he

did before he had died. His conscience and reason still operated (verse 24). He had his memory (verse 25), and affectionate feelings (verses 27-28). And his powers of imagination were working (verse 30). Undoubtedly, if the lost possessed these qualities in hell, the saved must also possess them in Paradise.

Paul knew that upon death he would immediately be with Christ, and the blessedness would be so great that he longed to go: "having a desire to depart, and to be with Christ; which is far better" (Philippians 1:23). And he further declared triumphantly, "to die is gain" (Philippians 1:21). From these verses we can know that your little girl is now in Paradise, in the presence of God, and is *better off* than when she was here!

This is a great consolation for, although she cannot return to you, you can live in such a way that some day you can go to her (II Samuel 12:23). In Paradise she can never sin and be lost. If she had not died, there is always the chance that she might sin, then die and be lost. But now she is forever safe, in a place where sin can never touch her.

If your other daughters had died, being unsaved they would have gone to hell. But God spared them and they still have opportunity to repent and go to heaven.

You see, it was the goodness of God that He took your sweet child to be with Himself and be forever safe from the devil's power and from hell. And it was His mercy that He did not take your unsaved daughters. Now they can obey God's plan of salvation (Acts 2:38). Wouldn't it be better for you all to be reunited in heaven than for some to be lost in hell?

Then too, your little girl's going to be with Jesus gives

you the added incentive to make it in yourself so that you may be with the little one you love throughout eternity.

So God knew exactly what He was doing in taking your little girl. Instead of resentfulness filling your heart, thank Him that she is forever safe and waiting for you. Instead of brooding, let praise fill your heart. Your task now is to so live that you will be able to win your two unsaved daughters to the Lord.

••••••••••••

"How Can I Know God's Will?"

QUESTION:

In the last three years my husband and I have been through a lot, and I don't understand why. I can't seem to get an answer from God. When one makes a move in faith and loses all, how can you know if you are out of the will of God, or still in His will? I think that being in the will of God is the most important thing.

ANSWER:

I feel for you in your trouble, and pray that God will strengthen and sustain you through your trial. His grace is always sufficient. Never doubt His love for you. Trust Him, and He will bring you through victoriously.

I certainly agree that being in the will of God is vital to the Christian. However, many Christians fail to understand what being in the will of God consists of; they look at events that happen as indications as to whether or not they are in the will of God. This is the foolish concept of

Job's so-called "comforters" who accused Job of committing some horrible sin or being a hypocrite because of the terrible calamities that befell him. Yet Job was perfectly in the will of God the whole time.

God wants us to understand His will (Ephesians 5:17). Paul prayed without ceasing for the saints at Colosse that they "might be filled with the knowledge of his will in all wisdom and spiritual understanding; That [they] might walk worthy of the Lord unto all pleasing. . ." (Colossians 1:9-10).

We might divide the scriptural teaching of the will of God into two headings: the *general* will of God, and the *specific* (or personal) will of God. Most people think of the latter when they speak of the will of God. Yet we cannot know the specific or personal will of God for our lives until first the general will of God is fulfilled in us. If we leap ahead and try to find the specific will of God before we have submitted ourselves to do the general will of the Lord, God will point us right back to the general. Only after we have obeyed Him in the general area will the specific will of God be opened up to us.

An excellent example of the general will of God is found in I Thessalonians 4:3-8, which begins by saying, "For this is the will of God, even your sanctification." Sanctification means, as the *Amplified Version* renders it, "separated and set apart for pure and holy living." If you have not surrendered yourself to God and allowed sanctification to be fulfilled in you, there is no need for you to ask God to reveal His will to you in any other specific way. The general will of God must come first in your life.

Another example of the general will of God is I Thessalonians 5:18: "In everything give thanks: for this is the will of God in Christ Jesus concerning you." If you cannot praise and thank God for all things He has permitted in your life, knowing and believing that Romans 8:28 is true, then any further unfolding of a specific will of God for your life will be blocked by your unbelief.

When you have allowed these two examples of the general will of God to be fulfilled in you, then you are ready for God to begin opening up specific lines of direction for your life.

Psalm 37 tells us in verse 23 that "the steps of a good man are ordered by the LORD." These steps are given in verses 3 to 7 in this order: (1) Trust in the LORD (verse 3), confident of His direction; (2) Delight thyself in the LORD (verse 4), allowing Him to fill your very being with His presence and joy; (3) Commit thy way unto the LORD (verse 5), having no will of your own but completely surrendering it all to Him; and finally (4) Rest in the Lord (verse 7), knowing He loves you and will direct you.

It might be that step 3 is the most difficult, for we all seem to want to tell the Lord what we want to do and then ask Him to bless it, instead of allowing Him to direct us into His way. Yet we will never have His direction until we completely put the matter entirely into His hands. Madame Guyon said,

"If place we seek, or place we shun
The soul finds happiness in none;
But with the Lord to guide our way
This equal joy to go or stay."

In *My Father's House,* the book for the new convert's

course offered by the Home Missions Division of the United Pentecostal Church, the following very revealing guide to knowing the specific will of God is given.

An excellent guide in knowing a proper sense of direction for your life is the following "Sense Test." When all four areas are affirmatively aligned, we can be assured of God's guidance.

1. Does it make common sense? Would God have you do something that was utterly ridiculous and logically unreasonable?

2. Does it make Bible sense? Would God have you do something that was contrary to His written Word?

3. Does it make Spirit sense? Would God have you do do something without the assurance of His Presence in it?

4. Does it make circumstancial sense? Would God have you do something that repeatedly encountered adverse circumstances?

God will go out of His way to make it perfectly clear to you what direction He is pointing. How can we be sure? He loves us, that's why! He knows we need His help. He is anxious to give it if we will but meet His conditions.

God listens to our petitions, like a father! Just be mindful that an answer from the Lord is still an answer. . . whether the response is yes, no, or wait! Sometimes we forget this. We have difficulty accepting answers as "from the Lord" if they are contrary to our desires.

This book, *My Father's House,* concludes the chapter with this paragraph.

Living in the will of God is not just trusting Him for the major events of our lives, it is living a life committed to His will every day. As the years go by, a life lived daily in God's will, will eventually result in a whole life lived in the will of God.

May I conclude by saying that prosperity is not necessarily a proof that one is in the will of God. If that were so, the rich people would be the most spiritual, which is most generally not true. (See Psalm 73.)

Neither is it true that adversity is proof that one is out of the will of God. We must all go through fiery trials to help purify us and prepare us for the Rapture. (See I Peter 4:12-13.)

But it is true that while we may "suffer according to the will of God" (I Peter 4:19), it is likewise true that "he that doeth the will of God abideth for ever" (I John 2:17). You cannot top that!

．．．．．．．．．．．．

The Cult of Personality

QUESTION:

I realize we are living in a new day, and I want end-time revival, but it seems like endtime revival has almost become the property of certain "glamor boys" who are slavishly followed nearly to the point of worship by some people. This new breed seems almost to flaunt their contempt for old-fashioned preaching and holiness, and to worship the god of success, numbers, prestige, and wealth. I am confused. What is happening?

ANSWER:

We have seen the rise, and in many cases the fall, of such superstars as A. A. Allen, William Branham, Oral Roberts, and T. L. Osborn. Before they appeared, we had others such as Aimee McPherson. Oneness people stood on the sidelines, maintained their integrity with God, and did not allow "the cult of personality" to delude us. We realized that our doctrine and power with God must center only in Jesus Christ; He must receive all the glory, and no individual must ever be exalted.

In Israel's day, after they had fought and won their great battles against the enemies of God and had settled down in the land of promise, "there arose another generation after them, which knew not the LORD" (Judges 2:10). These began to follow after "the gods of the people that were round about them" (verse 12).

Here is our danger. Great battles for pure doctrine and a separated life of holiness unto the Lord have been fought and won by our fathers. Today we have moved out of store fronts and brush arbors into lovely churches. We are possessing the land our fathers fought to give us.

Another generation has arisen. Many of them do not know or understand the tears, the battles, the groaning, the suffering, and the opposition their fathers went through. Nor do they possess the vision or the depth of consecration to the divine and perfect will of God of these giants for God of yesterday. They see the "success" of the leaders of "the cult of personality" in the religious world around them, and instead of "hating even the garment spotted by the flesh," they follow after the same gods of numbers, wealth, and prestige, just as the denominations do. Only now it is done in the name of "evangelism" or "endtime revival,"

This cuts a great swath, for a sensational personality impresses people because of the spectacular results. We exalt individuals because of their "success" and the result is that we begin to have "superstars" and worship gifts instead of God and follow charisma instead of Christ.

God's Word condemns the exaltation of individuals, those who have "men's persons in admiration because of advantage" (Jude 16). Pride lifts men up. The result is that some seem to think they have grown to a place where they are too big to follow "the old paths, the good way." The scriptural admonition, "submit yourselves one to another in the fear of God" (Ephesains 5:21), has no longer any place in their thinking. They feel they can do anything they want to and it is all right because they label it "evangelism" or "endtime revival." These things are of deep concern to spiritual and godly men today, including many of their own generation.

Yet others slavishly follow wherever the man of distinction and "success" leads. I have seen it happen that when an issue arises concerning holiness or ethics or doctrine, some foolish person will interject, "Well, look at Brother So-and-so. He is a great man and God is blessing him. He is doing it, so it must be all right." Instead of finding God's will by searching the Scriptures and seeking the face of God, they are swayed by a gifted personality, and they permit that personality to determine the will of God for them. Oh, how foolish!

Have we gotten to the place where we worship bigness, where we equate numbers and prosperity with God's favor and spirituality? If size and numbers were the criteria of success, we would all be foolish not to join the large denominations.

I have in my possession an old Methodist book given to my maternal grandfather by his mother in 1869. This book is entitled *Perfect Love,* by J. A. Wood, and published by the Methodist Episcopal Book Room in Philadelphia. The following excerpts all too graphically describe our present day Pentecostal movement—all that needs to be done is substitute the word *Pentecostal* for *Methodist.*

"The church has numbers, wealth, talents, and influence; but she needs something more than these—the power of the Holy Ghost, the gospel preached in the demonstration of the Spirit—the holy anointing from heaven.

"The Methodist church is in great danger of drifting away from her primitive simplicity, spirituality, and healthful discipline. It is believed by many that while she is increasing in numbers and becoming wealthy and popular, there are sad and unmistakable evidences that in many places she is losing her original zeal, sacrificing spirit, and spiritual power.

"When the Methodist church, or any other church, relies for her success upon any thing but deep, vital, and practical godliness, she will inevitably fail in accomplishing her great mission. Numbers, wealth, learning, position, or popularity, can never supply the place of piety. This is indispensable, and it must be first, last, and always.

"Was Mr. Wesley fearful that the people called Methodists would ever cease to be? I am not afraid that the people called Methodists should ever cease to exist. But I am afraid lest they should exist as a dead sect. And this un-

doubtedly will be the case unless they hold fast the doctrine, spirit, and discipline, with which they first set out. Mr. Wesley's clear spiritual vision saw the great point of danger to which the church was exposed, and feared that the spirit of plain, simple Methodism would depart from her, and that the spirit of the world would take its place.

"If Mr. Wesley were to leave his mansion near the throne and visit the Methodist churches of America in this day, we fear he would have occasion to cry out in the language of the venerable Asbury: Come back! COME BACK!! COME BACK!!!"

In spite of this warning and the warnings of others who saw the dangers of the drift Methodism was taking, the Methodist church did not come back. Undoubtedly in the days of J. A. Wood it was not too late. But look at her today! She is long gone from the simplicity, spirituality, and discipline of her early days.

But it is not too late with us although the hour is late. We must remember Proverbs 22:28: "Remove not the ancient landmarks, which thy fathers have set."

It is dangerous to be a personality follower, to be carried away by some individual "glamor boy" with charisma, or someone who claims some super-duper gift. Fall in love with Jesus, and don't join the last day, Laodicean "Cult of Personality."

•••••••••••

"Why Do My Sins Still Haunt Me?"

QUESTION:

I gave up my sins and asked Him to forgive me when I repented and asked Jesus to be my Lord and Savior. Then I was baptized in the name of Jesus Christ and received the Holy Ghost. Why is it that my sins still haunt me? Can it be that I haven't forgiven myself? Were my sins too shameful?

ANSWER:

The promise is sure: "If we confess our sins, he is faithful and just to forgive us our sins, and to cleanse us from all unrighteousness" (I John 1:9). The problem, then, is surely not with God's ability or willingness to forgive.

The only person left to doubt is yourself—which you have indeed done. So the question we need to answer is, "How can I learn to forgive myself, since I know that God already has forgiven?" Here are a few suggestions.

(1) *Turn your attention away from yourself.* You grow into Christ's likeness by beholding Him (II Corinthians 3:18), not by beholding yourself. As soon as you arise in the morning, fix your thoughts on Him. Read His Word, talk with Him. Let Him captivate your imagination so that you have no time to be doing mental replays of your past sins.

(2) *Discredit your feelings of guilt.* You may indeed have a sense of remorse for your past foolishness, and this is fitting. But the devil will try to transform those feelings of remorse into feelings of guilt and rejection. He would like to make your feelings of guilt so strong

94

that you forget Romans 8:1, "There is therefore now no condemnation to them which are in Christ Jesus. . . ." That promise is true, not because you feel it, but because God has promised it.

(3) *Imagine Peter during the night of Christ's capture and trial.* He has just denied his Lord. He is out in the darkness weeping, feeling the most awful weight of self-accusation and rejection. Write Peter a "letter" telling him the things he most needs to hear in his hour of grief, assuring him of Christ's love and forgiveness and acceptance. Then "mail" the letter to yourself. Put it in your Bible, read it often, and believe it. Can your sins be worse that Peter's?

(4) *Learn the beautiful secret of praise.* When unworthy thoughts come, start praising the Lord that He has forgiven you, that He has counted you worthy to bear His name, that He has seen fit to make your body His dwelling-place, that you are a child of God. You are free! Rejoice in it, thank and praise God for it, and you will find that it will become more and more real to you as you exercise your faith through praise. Refuse to acknowledge those past sins. They are gone forever. You grieve the Spirit of God when you bring them up, for in doing so you doubt the power of the blood. Praise will enable you to rise up over this and enter into the realm of faith and victory. Make this your testimony: "His praise shall continually be in my mouth" (Psalm 34:1).

Deathbed Repentance

QUESTION:

Is there not such a thing as deathbed repentance? How about the dying thief?

ANSWER:

There may be such a thing as deathbed repentance today, but do not depend on it. The dying thief was accepted, but he lived and died in a different dispensation than we do. Furthermore, probably it was the first and only chance he had ever had in his life to look to Jesus when he repented.

A person who lives in this enlightened day when the Bible is available everywhere, and when the gospel is preached throughout the land, simply has no excuse. To think that a man can reject the repeated calls of God and the many opportunities afforded him, and live for sin and the devil all his life until the last and escape all the consequences of a lifetime of sin, is simply not reasonable.

God must give repentance (II Timothy 2:25). How can one be sure God will grant repentance on any other than His time and terms? It is the height of folly to presume on such an unlikely eventuality. Proverbs 1:24-32 seems to indicate that God does not grant salvation after a lifetime of rejection.

•••••••••••

Is it Permissible to Use Physical Force?

QUESTION:

In view of verses of Scripture such as "the weapons of our warfare are not carnal" and "turn the other cheek," is it permissible to use physical force to protect yourself, wife, or children from harm?

ANSWER:

The position of the United Pentecostal Church relative to "Conscientious Scruples" as given in the Articles of Faith is as clear and scriptural a position as I have found anywhere. I suggest you obtain a copy and read it in its entirety. However, a portion of it is pertinent to your question as follows:

We recognize the institution of human government as being of divine ordination, and in so doing, affirm unanswering loyalty to our government; however, we take a definite position regarding the bearing of arms or the taking of human life.

As followers of the Lord Jesus Christ, the Prince of Peace, we believe in implicit obedience to His commandments and precepts which instruct us as follows: "that ye resist not evil" (Matthew 5:39); "follow peace with all men" (Hebrews 12:14). (See also Matthew 26:52; Romans 12:19; James 5:6; Revelation 13:10.) These we believe and interpret to mean Christians shall not shed blood nor take human life."

It is my conviction that this is referring primarily to suffering for Christ's sake or for the gospel's sake, and not to defending attacks against your wife or children.

I do think, however, that even in such an instance, which conceivably could happen but probably will not, there should be no thought of shedding blood. If necessity arose, purely a defensive or holding action should be taken, and only as much as is actually necessary.

But keep this in mind always: Your best defense is the Lord. A deeply spiritual man once said, "Nothing can happen to me outside of God's will, for I have put myself completely and entirely into His hands." When you do this you will know that He is your defense and your strong tower.

God's Word says, "They gather themselves together against the soul of the righteous, and condemn the innocent blood. But the LORD is my defence; and my God is the rock of my refuge. And he shall bring upon them their own iniquity, and shall cut them off in their own wickedness; yea, the LORD our God shall cut them off" (Psalm 94:21-23).

•••••••••••

Enlisting in the Military

QUESTION:
What is the church's stand on its people enlisting in the military and serving our country? The Bible says, "Those who live by the sword"; but it also says we are to be loyal to our country.

ANSWER:
There are two main reasons, I believe, why God has blessed our nation so greatly above all the other nations

of the earth.

It certainly is not because we are a godly nation. While we have the slogan, "In God We Trust," on our coins, actually the god America trusts in is represented by the coins themselves. The gods worshiped by most Americans are materialism, pleasure, popularity, self-indulgence, education, and success. And the churches that are supposed to be Christian actually preach another Jesus and another gospel that the apostles would never recognize. Promiscuity, license, and permissiveness predominate. No, America is not a godly nation.

Further, it is not because we are a moral nation that we are blessed; we are rapidly sinking to the depths of immorality. Even godless, heathen nations stand aghast at the sexual excesses and the openly immoral conduct of Americans. Our films are forbidden to be shown in many countries because of their lewdness. We are not a moral people.

Neither are we blessed because of our peacefulness. Rather, violence and crime are rapidly becoming the norm in America. Violent crimes continue to escalate alarmingly, touching ever-increasing numbers of households, including my own. One radical stated, "Violence is as American as apple pie." Murders, assassinations, rapes, and crimes against the person are everyday occurrences. Conduct is tolerated in America that is permitted in no other nation on earth. We are a violent people.

In spite of the lawlessness, uncleanness, and godlessness of our country, we have been (and still are) blessed, perhaps above all the nations of the earth. One reason God has smiled on us is that we have been a friend to God's earthly people Israel. God's promise to Abraham, "I will bless them that bless thee," still holds good. As long as we are a friend to the Jewish people, God will bless us.

The second reason we are so blessed is because America has provided a sanctuary and given complete liberty of conscience to God's people. We are a separate people, peculiar and unworldly. We do not fit in with the secular world and all their ways. We cannot participate with them in many of their activities and amusements. Yet America permits us to worship God as we choose, and this nation grants liberty of conscience in all areas of life that affect us.

In no area is this more pronounced than in the matter of bearing of arms and service in the armed forces of our nation. As a movement (although individuals may differ) the position of the United Pentecostal Church (with which I wholeheartedly concur) is that we may serve our country as loyal citizens in any and every capacity to which we may be called except in the "bearing of arms or the taking of human life" (Articles of Faith, *Manual of the United Pentecostal Church,* page 24). Our nation honors our conscientious scruples in this matter, and grants our people the right to this position. In times of war our young people have served with valor in many non-combatant capacities, some in positions of great hazard to their own lives.

If you will read the Article of Faith, "Conscientious Scruples," on page 24 of our *Manual,* and study the verses of Scripture listed, it will help you to understand our position and the position of God's Word revealing God's will for His church.

May I conclude with this excerpt from that article: "We therefore exhort our members to freely and willingly respond to the call of our government except in the matter of bearing arms. When we say service, we mean service, no matter how hard or dangerous. The true church has no more place for cowards than does the nation. First of all, however, let us earnestly pray that we will with honor be kept out of war. We believe that we can be consistent in serving our government in certain noncombatant capacities, but not in the bearing of arms."

．．．．．．．．．．．．

"My Problem is Self-Hatred"

QUESTION:

My problem is self-hatred. I have always had a terrible hatred of my looks (this is the main one), and myself in general. Premature aging runs in my family. Now that I am beginning to look much older than my friends, my last shred of self-esteem has been destroyed. These problems are damaging my marriage and my relationship with my children. I hope you can help me.

ANSWER:

Your problem is really not so rare as you may think. Few people are satisfied with themselves. There is a measure of self-pity in the natural make-up of all of us.

Really though, you do not hate yourself. You love yourself. In fact, you love yourself so much that you feel like you have been unfairly dealt with by "Mother Nature," that you do not deserve to be so mistreated. So you feel sorry for yourself and sink into a depression which has self-pity at the roots. It is difficult for you to recognize this, and even more difficult for you to acknowledge it. But it is only when you do that you will be able to rise up out of the slough of despond and begin your recovery. Your deliverance is in God.

There are those who feel that to have an inferiority complex is the essence of humility. Actually those with an inferiority complex are as proud or more so than those with a superiority complex. Both individuals have self as their center. Each has himself in his thoughts continually—always measuring himself and comparing himself with others. This is pride, not humility. The truly humble person is not one who thinks meanly of himself; actually he does not think of himself at all. He is not self-conscious, not self-centered, and does not indulge in either self-exaltation or self-pity. Self simply is not the center of his thoughts at all.

The spiritually healthy, happy individual is at peace with God, with others, and with himself. He has learned the grace of self-acceptance, that he is an individual made as God has desired him to be. Whatever shortcomings he may possess, whatever he may lack which others have, do not dismay him because he knows that God has made him with compensations. These he will use for God's glory and not bemoan the things which he may lack. He accepts himself.

Your failure is not your physical deformity, if you would call it that. To complain, to live in despair, depression and despondency—that is your failure. To complain is actually to blame God for what you consider your misfortune. Multitudes have afflictions far, far worse than yours who have learned to live happy, productive lives.

Their friends, acquaintances, and relatives never notice the physical infirmity because the beauty of their glowing spirit refreshes everyone around them.

It is not "premature aging" that is damaging your marriage and relationship with your children. Not at all! It is your unhealthy, unwholesome, carnal, self-centered attitude which magnifies a physical infirmity all out of proportion in your own eyes, until your miserable self-pity makes you a truly unlovable individual.

May I suggest you start praising and thanking God for your many blessings. Never permit yourself the luxury of wallowing in self-pity. Try Psalm 34:1 on for size: "I will bless the LORD at all times: his praise shall continually be in my mouth." God loves you and has blessed you with a multitude of blessings. Get your mind and your thoughts on these things. Accept what God allows in your life as God's will for you, and rejoice that you are a child of God. You have compensating talents which probably you have never used. Start using them. Forget yourself in blessing others.

Fill your heart with thanksgiving and your mouth with His praises, and believe me, your tomorrows will be far more wonderful than your yesterdays, no matter how old you may get!

•••••••••••

How to Keep From Being Deceived

QUESTION:

Many people have asked the question, "How can I know what is right and wrong?" In other words, they do not

103

want to be deceived. The following article is given to answer this question and to help a person avoid being deceived by false teachers and erroneous doctrines.

ANSWER:

Child of God, brace yourself! Dig down deep into God and His Word. Keep constantly filled with the Spirit. We have entered into a period just prior to the coming of the Lord for His bride, a time, the like of which God's church has never seen. It is the time spoken of by Paul when he said, "Evil men and seducers shall wax worse and worse, deceiving, and being deceived" (II Timothy 3:13).

The deluge has already begun! I mean the deluge of deceivableness with which this age will close. Great signs and wonders will be shown of such cunning deception that Jesus said, "If it were possible, they shall deceive the very elect" (Matthew 24:24). Multitudes of Pentecostal people will be deceived and swept away by it, and some already have. The magnitude of the deluge of deception and consequent departing from the faith will be so grievous that the Bible describes it as the "falling away" (II Thessalonians 2:3).

This time of great religious upheaval, of which both Jesus and the apostles prophesied, is now upon us. Do not boast that you cannot be taken in and deceived. It was Paul's constant fear that the Corinthian Christians would have their "minds. . .corrupted from the simplicity that is in Christ," even "as the serpent beguiled Eve" (II Corinthians 11:3). He feared the constant "brainwashing" power of the devil. This article is to help you know how to keep yourself from succumbing to the seductive deceptions of Satan.

Blind Leaders

It is impossible for the man without the Pentecostal Baptism of the Holy Ghost to teach another the spiritual truths of God's Word. Why? Because he does not understand them himself; though he may claim to, and actually believe that he does.

We are told in I Corinthians 2:14 that "the natural man [that is, the man who does not have the Holy Ghost] receiveth not the things of the Spirit of God." The reason simply is because he has not first of all received the Spirit itself. The verse further declares that it is impossible for him to know spiritual things because they are spiritually understood, or understood through the enlightenment which the Holy Ghost gives.

I would not sit under, nor give ear to, the ministry of one without the Holy Ghost baptism. He is not qualified to teach or to preach. He is blinded; he is off the track. He cannot know or understand spiritual things. He is a blind leader of the blind.

Be Filled With The Spirit

Jesus told His disciples that they were to be His witnesses throughout the earth, but first they were to tarry until they were endued with Holy Ghost power from on high. Then, Jesus said, "When he, the Spirit of truth, is come, he will guide you into all truth" (John 16:13). Thus we see that the man without the Holy Ghost does not have truth. He must first get the Holy Ghost and be led into the truth himself before he can preach or teach the truth to others.

Many are in this pitiful condition! Paul spoke of them in I Timothy 1:7, "Desiring to be teachers of the law;

understanding neither what they say, nor whereof they affirm." The simplest, most ignorant one with the Holy Ghost is more qualified to teach than they, no matter the amount of education they may have received. Though they may quote much Scripture, they do not have the necessary illumination of the Spirit of God to rightly divide the word of truth. Only the foolish and non-spiritual will listen to those having not the Spirit. To sit under their teaching is a sure way to be deceived. (See Romans 16:18.)

How can one keep from being deceived? It is a very important and an absolute necessity to listen only to those who are filled with the Holy Ghost according to the apostles' doctrine, whom God Himself has filled, called, trained, equipped, qualified, and set in the church to minister (I Corinthians 12:28). These Holy Ghost filled ministers are for the perfecting of the saints (Ephesians 4:12).

Paul said that we (the Spirit-filled ministry) have received the Spirit which is of God, that we might know the things that are freely given to us of God, and that God reveals those things to us by His Spirit, for the Spirit searcheth all things, yea, the deep things of God. Which things we (the Holy Ghost ministry) speak, not in the words which man's wisdom teacheth, but which the Holy Ghost teacheth. (See I Corinthians 2:10-12.)

You can only be safeguarded from being deceived as you keep Spirit-filled yourself, and listen and follow the Holy Ghost ministry God has put over you in the church. To listen to those without the Spirit is to surely be deceived. And to refuse to listen and obey your Spirit-filled and God-anointed minister is to be deceived, for God put him in the church to teach you and, by the Holy Ghost, to guide you into all the truth of God's Word.

The Holy Ghost church, led by the preaching of God's holy Word by the Spirit-filled ministry, is the pillar and ground of the truth (I Timothy 3:15). "All other ground is sinking sand!"

Crucify The Flesh

One of the greatest enemies the child of God has is self, or flesh. The terms are scripturally synonymous. And the fleshly or carnal mind is, we are told in Romans 8:7, "enmity against God; for it is not subject to the law [Word] of God."

The fleshly or carnal mind, the mind of self, opposes the mind of the Spirit controlling your life. (See Galatians 5:17.) It is a war to the death! For a child of God to yield to carnal reasoning or self-will, is to open his mind to delusion of the worst sort. For this deception is self-deception, that which the human nature believes because it wants to believe. It is easy, pleasant, and soothing to the natural man to believe those things which spare him.

But the Word of God, to which the carnal mind is not subject, reveals that the child of God must crucify the flesh. Self-will must be destroyed! For self-will leads to self-delusion; and self-delusion, to strong delusion. Let me give you an example. God's Word says to forsake not assembling together (Hebrews 10:25), because the work of the ministry is "for the perfecting of the saints," to bring God's people unto "the knowledge of the Son of God, unto a perfect man, unto the measure of the stature of the fulness of Christ" (Ephesians 4:11-13).

But the carnal mind, not subject to the Word of God, says, "Stay at home and read the Bible there. You can

107

study your own way and teach yourself." Very soon this man's undisciplined, unguided and unguarded mind, having yielded to this self-exalting delusion, will be receiving other false and destructive ideas contrary to sound doctrine.

He may actually boast that he is free and led of the Spirit, but in reality he has become a slave of the worst sort, dominated by his carnal mind, a prey to all false and damning doctrines, and wandering farther and farther astray. Self-will has destroyed him, leading to self-delusion and eventually a strong delusion and he is damned while claiming to be saved.

I have seen this happen. I have seen potentially outstanding workers of God make shipwreck through self-will, because they would not be subject to the ministry and the Word of God.

King Saul's self-will led him to presumptuous worship of his own, apart from Samuel's direction. Later on, that same self-will caused him to go according to his carnal mind against the word of God's prophet in sparing King Agag. This self-will resulted in his complete and utter abandonment by God, and he eventually sought guidance from a witch. His end was tragic, a horrible example of the fearful cost of one who would not be teachable and submissive to the ministry and the Word of God.

Oh, friend, maintain a teachable, humble spirit. Crucify the flesh with its affections and lusts. Bring every thought into obedience to Christ and His Word. Let not self, so soft, comfortable, and enticing, lure you away from the narrow way of full surrender to God. My friend, learn to deny self. If you don't, you will surely be deceived sooner or later. If you do, you will keep from being deceived.

Faithfully Attend Your United Pentecostal Church

God's Word speaks of some who are "never able to come to the knowledge of the truth" (II Timothy 3:7). Here is a picture of those who are deceived and blinded. The context in verses 6 and 7 describes creatures as "silly," "captives," "sin-laden," "controlled by their own lustful desires," and "always learning, but unable to find the truth." What a horrible picture! Deceived! Blinded! Deluded! Hell-bound!

But why are they deceived? Does it not say they are ever learning? Why then isn't it possible for them to learn the truth? Isn't there hope for those who learn?

Ah, but wait! These are called "wandering stars" (Jude 13), searching for teachers with itching ears, never established, never grounded, unstable as water, wishwashy. They are as foolish children at a carnival, wandering around from one unsanitary vendor to another, nibbling on this and that; eating popcorn, hot dogs, cotton candy, ice-cream, hamburger, taffy, potato chips; drinking pink lemonade and soda pop, and then wondering why they have a king-sized stomachache.

At home mother can prepare the finest and most delicious dinner, filled with health-giving vitamins, but the children's faces are green with indigestion and nausea. Their stomachs are filled with totally indigestible trash and they have no appetite for good food. Just so, those who are "ever learning" wander from teacher to teacher, and from church to church and are "never able to come to the knowledge of the truth," for they are so filled with trash, foolishness, half-truths, and fables, that they have no appetite for the "sound doctrine" or the milk and meat of God's Word.

We are told that because they do not have a love for the truth (preferring to nibble here and there from religious hucksters), God will send them a strong delusion. They will believe a lie and be damned (II Thessalonians 2:10-12).

O my friend, do not just let any man teach you! God's Word says to "know them which labour among you" (I Thessalonians 5:12). It is fatal to receive teaching from just any source. Steer clear of everything and everyone that is not proven to be fully and completely apostolic, and in harmony with our brethren in the United Pentecostal Church. That is the only safe course in these treacherous days of apostasy. Even if an angel should appear, all bright and shining, though he talk with the tongues of men and angels, if he doesn't preach or teach the apostolic doctrine of one God, new birth, and holiness, flee from him as you would a plague! He is accursed! (See Galatians 1:8-9.) Even to invite him into your house, or to bid him God-speed, is to become partaker with him in his damnation. (See II John 9-11.)

Your safety lies in abiding in the truth that you have been taught as it is in Christ Jesus. Eat regularly the good, sound, wholesome, appetizing, well-balanced meals of God's Word as it is served to you in God's house. This is the only way to keep from being deceived.

Wolves In Sheep's Clothing

There is much that is spectacular today—much that emphasizes the external, the dramatic, and the sensational. Dripping blood, stigmata, crosses of gold, oil, wine, or manna mysteriously appearing on hands, leaping flames of fire, toads in bottles which supposedly are demons cast out of people, are only a few. And these mysterious things are put forward as evidences of divine favor and power resting upon those who claim such things. But are we to accept these claims as from God? Are these evidences that God gives to those who are His chosen?

Listen to what Jesus said in Matthew 7:15-16: "Beware of false prophets, which come to you in sheep's clothing, but inwardly they are ravening wolves. Ye shall know them by their fruits. Do men gather grapes of thorns, or figs of thistles?"

External appearances can be very deceptive. We are told in II Corinthians 11:14-15 that Satan himself is transformed into an angel of light, and his ministers into ministers of righteousness. So external evidences are unreliable. A false prophet will appear to be a sheep externally, for he will disguise himself in sheep's clothing and claim great power and holiness. But unseen, they are vicious, ravening wolves, deceiving gullible, unstable souls.

How then can we detect the false prophet? Jesus said, "Ye shall know them by their fruits." We are told in I Thessalonians 5:12 to "know them which labour among you, and are over you in the Lord, and admonish you."

Too often when an unknown individual arises, producing sensational and spectacular things, foolish people flock to see, hear, and follow such a leader. No wonder they are deceived and deluded and doomed.

But wise, spiritual, godly people "prove all things," and look underneath the gaudy front to see the background and character of the man, that they may know him before they follow him. And, too, they patiently wait to see what kind of fruit he produces before they will accept his wares. It takes time to produce fruit, but Jesus said to wait and see and examine the fruit before accepting the ministry of such a one.

Fruit Is The Test

Fruit is the test. If a man rebels against truth, against God's ministry and church, and then proclaims greater power or holiness, he is a liar and a deceiver. He is a false prophet. It makes no difference if he is a "miracle worker," if he prays, if he weeps, if he preaches like an angel. These are the sheep's clothing he wears. But inwardly he is a ravening wolf.

There have been those who left our fellowship rather than line up to the truth and doctrine of God's Word. Others have been rebellious, disobedient, and self-exalted. Still others are not willing to live a separated life of holiness unto God. Some have borrowed money and still owe it to some of the saints. Some were not willing to dress right, act right, talk right. They said we were too strict.

You can find these people now in false doctrines, deceived, deluded, and doomed. Their fruits tell on them. The churches that have "swallowed them down" are false churches, wolves in sheep's clothing. Yet many now claim-superior holiness, spectacular and fantastic gifts, external manifestations of all kinds. But Jesus said,"By their fruits ye shall know them."

Jesus used the word *beware*. It is a strong word. It is a word used to warn one against a vicious animal. It is dangerous to play with false or doubtful doctrines. It is equally as dangerous to blindly accept flattery and attention and outward manifestations of "love." Beware!

Beware!

Beware of the spectacular and sensational, not plainly taught in God's Word. Beware of all that is not proven, known, and time-tested, even though it may appear as a miraculous angel from heaven.

Beware! Hold off! Prove all things! Wait for the fruit, then examine it closely. Remember, Jesus said, "By their fruits ye shall know them."

Love The Truth

God's Word warns that "because they received not the love of the truth, that they might be saved. . .they should believe a lie. That they all might be damned who believed not the truth" (II Thessalonians 2:10-12).

Plainly, those who refuse to believe the truth will be lost. The devil hates the truth. Jesus said, "Ye shall know the truth and the truth shall make you free" (John 8:32). Truth delivers, truth liberates, truth saves. Only worship which is in Spirit and in the truth is accepted by God (John 4:24). Truth is God (John 14:6). To reject truth is to reject God; to accept truth is to accept God; therefore, "Buy the truth and sell it not" (Proverbs 23:23). Truth is worth more than all the world.

It is here that the devil wars against the souls of men. "Yea, hath God said?" is still the seducing appeal of Satan, even as it was to Eve. And Paul wrote in II Corinthians 11:3, "I fear, lest by any means, as the serpent beguiled Eve through his subtilty, so your minds should be corrupted from the simplicity that is in Christ." Again, Paul says, "If our gospel be hid, it is hid to them that are lost: In whom the god of this world hath blinded the minds of them which believe not" (II Corinthians 4:4).

Let no seducing, enticing, subtle spirit beguile you away from the truth. John said, "We are of God: he that knoweth God heareth us; he that is not of God heareth not us. Hereby know we the spirit of truth, and the spirit of error" (I John 4:6).

Ask God to give you a love for the truth. Your salvation depends on it. Not mere grudging acceptance or unwilling toleration, but a genuine love, a love that will not compromise or bend; a strong, firm, hot love that cleaves to the truth with a passionate, fixed devotion.

Truth is not flexible; it does not waver. It is fixed as the stars in their orbits. It is right yesterday, and today, and it will be right forever. If the apostles preached it, cleave to it; if they didn't, it is not truth. Abhor the false as you would poison. (See Galatians 1:8-9.)

O, my friend, simply believe God, believe His Word, believe His truth, believe it the most when it crosses your reason and your desires. Believe it when you don't understand it. Believe it when it is argued against with convincing arguments. Believe it—believe it all. Cling to it without wavering, or you will be lost!

3

Holiness

Falling Away from Holiness

QUESTION:

I recently read in my Bible about a "falling away" that would take place in the last days. I asked a friend of mine what this meant and he said it refers to Christian nations being taken over by godless communism. But I wonder if it does not refer to the fact that many of our people are forsaking holiness, getting TV's, dressing "mod," and some of our churches even having recreation rooms with pin-ball machines and bowling alleys, and using TV to advertise. Some may even allow their youth to go to professional ballgames and skating rinks. What is happening among us today? Aren't we falling away from the standards of our godly heritage and becoming just like the denominational world? Where is the separation? Where is the Cross? I would appreciate your comments.

ANSWER:

While I do not hold with the idea that the "falling away" of II Thessalonians 2:3 refers necessarily to the church of our day, nor do I agree with the interpretation of your friend, I do look with sadness upon the tendency of some among us to abandon the standards of holiness that brought us where we are today.

These things are not only deeply troubling to me, but to others also of our ministers who may be called of the "old school" that love the narrow way. There are occasions when godly ministers have been held up to ridicule because they preach against the things to which you refer. There seems to be a new, brazen, arrogant breed who care not one whit whether they bring a stumblingblock into their brother's way. They will do as they please and still desire the protective cloak of religiosity under the banner of the United Pentecostal Church.

Your list is by no means exhaustive. Much more could be added. But really, these worldly activities are but symptoms and not the disease itself. The disease is of the spirit. I am reminded of the words of J. A. Wood written in 1861 concerning the Methodist Church of his day: "I believe there is a class of temporizing, tobacco-chewing and cigar-smoking ministers getting into the pulpit who neither preach nor enjoy much religion, but are ever ready to utter an accusation against any who may profess or preach Christian holiness" (*Perfect Love*, p. 269). The same spirit behind the "tobacco-chewing and cigar-smoking ministers" of his day is behind those of our day who would compromise the precious truth of separation and bring worldly practices into our churches and into the lives of our people.

The old, many-times disproven argument that it is necessary to have these worldly attractions to hold our young people is simply the excuse of a spiritually sick minister. What is wrong with the Holy Ghost and fire that it cannot hold our young people? Let our services be mightily endued with divine power and we will hold our young people.

J. A. Wood proposes and then eloquently answers an important question: "How is a compromising spirit with the world usually manifested?" He said, "It manifests itself in many ways, some of which are the following:

"(1) In efforts to popularize Christianity with the world, and looking to increase her influence in that way.

118

"(2) In efforts to lower the Bible standard of piety in order to make it less repulsive to the minds of carnal men.

"(3) In efforts to regulate sin, instead of opposing and prohibiting it.

"(4) In acts which pander to the vices of wicked men, or which countenance, directly or indirectly, the commission of sin.

"(5) In the abandonment of Bible terms in the relation of religious experience, in order to please men.

"(6) In the polishing and softening of those truths which God has left rough and hard.

"(7) In depending for the prosperity of the church upon her wealth and popularity, or upon the learning, talents, and eloquence of her ministers, rather than upon the baptism of the Holy Ghost, and a solid, high tone of piety in her ministry and membership" (*Perfect Love*, pp. 255-256).

Jesus never bribed people to follow Him; He challenged them! He brought out the best that is in them. In our weak-kneed way, we try to bribe people; we offer them inducements borrowed from the world. But those we get by this means will always be weak and sickly. Compromise breeds compromise, and weakness breeds more weakness. The result? A flabby, sickly, anemic church. Oh yes, there may be some added to our number, but they will never be of the caliber or the fibre of normal New Testament saints.

Let me illustrate this with the experience of one of God's great men, Abraham. God had promised him a son when both he and his wife were long past the age of childbearing. Furthermore, Sarah had been barren all her life. So the fulfillment of this promise would depend upon two mighty supernatural acts of God: healing Sarah's barrenness and imparting youthful fertility to this elderly couple, ages 90 and 100 respectively.

Somehow Sarah was unable to grasp this promise. She laughed in unbelief at the very thought. Yet when she saw that her husband was determined to believe that he would have a son, she groped for a method to bring about the desired result without total dependence upon God's supernatural power. Sarah adopted a heathen, worldly practice and brought it over into their sanctified, separated, godly home. She convinced Abraham that by taking to his bosom a substitute woman, thus violating the God-ordained, sacred relationship of a monogamous marriage, he would have his son.

The result? Ishmael was born, the offspring of an unholy liaison between a godly man and a heathen woman. This birth has brought perpetual sorrow and anguish to God's nation of Israel, resulting even today in the present agony and bloodshed between the Jews and the Arabs.

Let the promised son be revival. Let Abraham represent God's church, Sarah those whom God desires to bless with revival but who are unwilling to go God's way to get it. Watch what they are doing. They are convincing the church to try the substitute, the heathen woman, worldly methods. Instead of the promised revival, another kind of son is born, a worldly, carnal, fleshly, and unspiritual offspring.

Those who make a god of numbers shout with glee. They say as Abraham, "O that Ishmael might live before thee!" (Genesis 17:18). But God rejected Ishmael. He accepts only that which He does in us and through us by His supernatural power.

No good thing ever comes of bringing worldly methods and practices into God's church. Instead of helping God out, we miss out on the blessedness God intended, and the result is always tragic.

The promised son, Isaac, a true Holy Ghost revival, will come only when we repudiate all carnal, man-made methods, ideas, and practices, and flee to God and the way of holiness. A supernatural birth will take place, and there will be a true revival.

Let us pray that God will help our precious people in the United Pentecostal Church to "ask for the old paths, where is the good way, and walk therein, and we shall find rest for our souls" (Jeremiah 6:16).

••••••••••••

Standards of Holiness

QUESTION:

You are probably one of the few narrow-minded preachers left who hold to the old, outmoded line of rigid "standards of holiness" as you call them. But to arbitrarily condemn innocent amusements and label them as "worldly" is adding to the Scriptures and becoming like the Pharisees, which Jesus condemned. If a person has the Holy Ghost in him, the Spirit will direct him, and he does not need carnal commandments (rules of conduct) any longer. (See I John 2:27 and Hebrews 7:16.) Your comment please.

ANSWER:

I do not find in my Bible where Jesus condemned the Pharisees for labeling "innocent amusements as worldly." It was their hypocrisy that Jesus uncovered and rebuked. Let us notice what Jesus told them:

> *"The scribes and the Pharisees sit in Moses' seat: All therefore whatsoever they bid you observe, that observe and do; but do ye not after their works: for they say, and do not. For they bind heavy burdens and grievous to be borne, and lay them on men's shoulders; but they themselves will not move them with one of their fingers. But all their works they do for to be seen of men" (Matthew 23:2-5).*

Nowhere in the Bible is a clean, separated walk with God condemned. It was because the Pharisees were not separated from sin when they claimed to be that Jesus indicted them.

> *"Woe unto you, scribes and Pharisees, hypocrites! for ye make clean the outside of the cup and of the platter, but within they are full of extortion and excess. Thou blind Pharisee, cleanse first that which is within the cup and platter, that the outside of them may be clean also. . . .Even so ye also outwardly appear righteous unto men, but within ye are full of hypocrisy and iniquity" (Matthew 23:25-26, 28).*

Jesus did not tell the Pharisees that the outside of

the cup and platter did not matter; rather He told them to cleanse first the inside "that the outside of them might be clean also."

Your argument that the Spirit alone is our guide is false. If it were true, we might as well throw our Bible away!

The Bible is filled with instructions and warnings against worldly indulgences. Paul wrote many of his epistles to correct the conduct of saints who had received the Holy Ghost. If the Spirit is all that is needed to direct an individual, much of the New Testament would never have been written.

One of the commands of God's Word to the ministry is that they are to "reprove, rebuke, exhort with all longsuffering and doctrine" (II Timothy 4:2). If the Spirit does this automatically, the ministry certainly would not have been told to do it. I am afraid the god of the world has blinded your eyes, friend. You need to "anoint thine eyes with eyesalve, that thou mayest see" (Revelation 3:18).

Your interpretation of the Scriptures to substantiate your false premises indicates a lack of basic Bible understanding. For in Hebrews 7:16, "carnal commandment" has no reference whatsoever to "rules of conduct." It is easy to see that it refers to the law given on Mt. Sinai. Verse 19 explains, "For the law made nothing perfect, but the bringing in of a better hope did; by the which we draw nigh unto God."

I John 2:27 has been the plaything of carnally-minded people who think that this one verse of Scripture cancels out all the hundreds of other verses that teach us that God has given pastors and teachers to the church for their perfection. Far from doing that, this verse means that we are not to allow men to teach us who are not filled and anointed with the Spirit of God. If you are truly filled with the Holy Ghost, that Spirit will confirm the teachings of the Spirit-filled minister to you.

We should notice what Paul wrote to the church in Corinth about this matter.

> *"If any man think himself to be a prophet, or spiritual, let him acknowledge that the things that I write unto you are the commandments of the Lord. But if any man be ignorant, let him be ignorant" (I Corinthians 14:37-38).*

There are many truly "innocent amusements" in which a child of God may safely participate. But God's true ministry, His "watchmen on the walls," will faithfully warn against those things which are not so innocent, but are traps of sin set for the unwary.

It appears that you desire to indulge in some activities that are not wholesome, and therefore you resent the warning of the true man of God. You do so at your peril. You have condemned yourself.

In closing, I am happy to say that you are wrong when you say that there are only a few of us left who love holiness. Perhaps in terms of the total population of the world, "few" is accurate, but this "few" includes hundreds of thousands in the wonderful fellowship of God's people who hold to standards that define their separation from worldliness, including the vast majority of the United Pentecostal Church International.

In fact, I believe God could repeat again what He said

to Elijah when this prophet felt that he was the only one left who stayed true to God; "I have. . .seven thousand. . . which have not bowed unto Baal" (I Kings 19:18). God's "seven thousand" people on the narrow way that leads unto life are greater in might and glory than the vast multitude of people on the broad way that leads to destruction.

•••••••••••

Rules of Conduct Are Necessary

QUESTION:

My pastor has begun to teach that we do not need rules governing our conduct, and that once we are saved we are secure, since it is only God's grace that saves us, not our goodness. He derides standards of holiness as bondage leading us back under legalism that Jesus delivered us from. He further says that sin will not keep us out of heaven. Would you care to comment?

ANSWER:

I am sorry to hear that a minister teaches doctrines borrowed from the denominational world that Pentecost has freed us from. The teachings you describe in your letter are contrary to the teachings of the Bible and of the United Pentecostal Church.

In the Articles of Faith of the United Pentecostal Church, on page 24 of our Manual under the title "The Grace of God," we read these words:

> *"A Christian, to keep saved, must walk with God and keep himself in the love of God (Jude 21) and in the grace of God. The word **grace** means "favor." When a person transgresses and sins against God, he loses His favor. If he continues to commit sin and does not repent, he will eventually be lost and cast into the lake of fire. (Read John 15:2, 6; II Peter 2:20, 21.) Jude speaks of the backsliders of his day and their reward. (Also, read Hebrews 6:4-6.)"*

One of the teachings you describe is known as "Unconditional Eternal Security," also called "once saved, always saved" or "once in grace, always in grace." It is taken from the teachings of John Calvin, one of the leaders of the Reformation, and it forms the theological base for the Reformed Church, Presbyterian Church, and the Baptist churches. Since it makes allowances for a person to sin without losing his salvation it has become very popular, especially with carnally minded people who do not want to live a holy, separated life. While we do not say that all who subscribe to this teaching necessarily do so in order to excuse their sin, nevertheless it has that effect.

John R. Rice, an ardent Calvinist on this point, in one of his famous passages describes how he envisions it will be at the Rapture by stating that many a David who has a Bathsheba sitting on his lap will rise to meet the Lord while Bathsheba falls off onto the ground. Or if a "Christian" is stealing a sack of potatoes, at the Rapture the "Christian" will go up releasing the sack of potatoes to fall and scatter. "So we may expect," he concludes, "the roofs of motion picture houses to need repair, broken by raptured but ashamed Christians when Jesus comes."

How completely unscriptural this all is!

There are many verses of Scripture which refute this teaching, too many to go into in the short space we have. But below are a few which effectively show the fallacy of "eternal security":

> *"We. . .beseech you also that ye receive not the grace of God in vain"* *(II Corinthians 6:1).*
>
> *"Christ is become of no effect unto you [who seek to be justified by the law]; . . .ye are fallen from grace"* *(Galatians 5:4).*
>
> *"I declare unto you the gospel. . .By which also ye are saved, if ye keep in memory what I preached unto you, unless ye have believed in vain"* *(I Corinthians 15:1-3).*
>
> We are the house of Christ *"if we hold fast. . .firm unto the end"* *(Hebrews 3:6).*
>
> *"We are made partakers of Christ, if we hold the beginning of our confidence stedfast unto the end"* *(Hebrews 3:14).*
>
> *"If God spared not the natural branches [Jews], take heed lest he also spare not thee. Behold therefore the goodness, and severity of God. . .toward thee, goodness if thou continue in his goodness: otherwise thou also shalt be cut off"* *(Romans 11:21-22).*

The people who teach unconditional eternal security refer continually to the grace of God and say that we who oppose this teaching do not really believe in the grace of God and are trying to be saved by works. But the grace of God does not teach us that sinning is acceptable to God.

Rather, grace teaches holy living. Titus 2:11-12 tells us that "the grace of God that bringeth salvation. . .teach[es] us that, denying ungodliness and worldly lusts, we should live soberly, righteously, and godly, in this present world."

In addition to "favor," grace means "the power God gives us to fulfill the will of God in our lives." In the light of this definition it is impossible to use grace as a crutch upon which to base the ungodly and pernicious teachings of Calvinism. Rather, grace gives us the power through the Holy Ghost to live a holy life. Saying that grace will permit us to sin belittles the power of the Holy Ghost, the very grace the false teacher claims to exalt!

The scriptural teaching of the security of the believer is not unconditional, but it is wonderful and reassuring. As long as you keep Jesus filling your heart, you are just as secure as if you are already in heaven. No man can pluck you out of His hand as long as you hear His voice and follow Him (John 10:27-29). But the false teaching that makes security unconditional removes from man the power of his free choice and the consequences of sin, which is separation from God, and which is taught everywhere in the Scriptures, such as I Corinthians 6:9-10.

This pernicious teaching has resulted in many people becoming loose and careless in their moral life. Some who once lived holy lives now say, "No matter what I do I can't be lost for I have once tasted of the grace of God." Every doctrine which is not conducive to a holy walk with God should be rejected, for verses of Scripture such as Hebrews 12:14 teach us that nobody can get to heaven without living a holy life.

If we do not have an intense, burning, red-hot love for God's truth, we are in serious danger. II Thessaloniano 2:10 12 warns us of the results. Those who receive not a love of the truth will believe a lie and be damned. A teaching that one can sin and still be saved qualifies for the kind of a lie that will lead one into damnation.

It saddens me to think of the dire results this pernicious teaching of unconditional eternal security has upon church people. It not only gives a false sense of security but it opens the door to careless and carnal living. Let us pray that such a standard of holiness be raised, and such straight, clean, holy preaching of the Word be proclaimed that it will put to flight all such false teachings.

•••••••••••

Pharisaism and Outward Holiness

QUESTION:

Are we not in danger of hypocrisy and Pharisaism such as Jesus condemned in Matthew 23:25-28 when we preach strong standards of dress and outward appearance, and emphasize that this is what "holiness" consists of? It seems to me that Jesus stressed the vital importance of first cleansing the inside. Surely inward cleansing is what true holiness consists of, and not an undue over-emphasis on external appearances. I am fearful that we may create a generation of Pharisees when we equate "holiness" with outward appearance. I am equally fearful that this generation of Pentecostals will never know what true holiness is. What a tragedy! Please comment.

ANSWER:

The passage of Scripture you refer to reads as follows:

> *"Woe unto you, scribes and Pharisees, hypocrites! for ye make clean the outside of the cup and of the platter, but within they are full of extortion and excess. Thou blind Pharisee, cleanse first that which is within the cup and platter, that the outside of them may be clean also. Woe unto you, scribes and Pharisees, hypocrites! for ye are like unto whited sepulchres, which indeed appear beautiful outward, but are within full of dead men's bones, and of all uncleanness. Even so ye also outwardly appear righteous unto men, but within ye are full of hypocrisy and iniquity"* (Matthew 23:25-28).

I sympathize with your point of view. It undoubtedly is true that in some places and occasions the pendulum has swung to an unwarranted degree toward undue emphasis on externals.

However, I certainly do not believe Jesus intended for us to neglect externals. In fact, Jesus emphasized in verse 26 that we are to clean first the inside "that the outside of them may be clean also." He wants both inside and outside clean.

We need to get the divine order right. Clean *first* the inside. That is where we must start, but that is not the end. That is the most important, but we must not stop with that. I do not think we should cease preaching against indecent attire, but I do think we should preach more against indecent thoughts and unclean hearts. If we can get people's hearts right and clean up the immodesty on the inside, it will be easy to straighten them out on their immodesty of dress.

Holiness is not merely adding inches onto a mini-skirt until it covers the knees; it is being partakers of God's holiness (Hebrews 12:10); it is being filled with His *Holy* Spirit and permitting Him to fully have His way in one's life. Outward conformity to holiness standards of dress will inevitably follow when the heart has holiness in it, and the one with true inward holiness will shun wearing unholy or immodest apparel.

While it is true that one may wear long skirts, be fully covered and look "saintly" and yet be hypocritical and pharisaical with a filthy mind and spirit, it is equally true that if one is inwardly holy, that holiness will seek to manifest itself in a godly and modest outward appearance.

The answer is to do as Jesus said, "Cleanse *first* the inside," to put the initial strong emphasis on holiness of heart; then as the inside is made holy it will desire outward manifestations of that holiness reigning within. Guidelines and standards of dress should be preached to enable that one to know how to fulfill his holy desires in outward appearance. To preach standards of dress is absolutely necessary in these days of lukewarmness and compromise. But put first things first. Thus the proper balance as Jesus gave it is achieved, and there will be little danger of hypocrisy and Pharisaism.

．．．．．．．．．．．．

"Rules" and "Bondage"

QUESTION:

Why do our churches have so many rules? I get so frustrated when new rules are handed down to us. I thought getting the Holy Ghost set us free from man-made rules and bondage, but it seems like I am in more bondage now than I was before I was saved. Why cannot the Bible be the only rule we need?

ANSWER:

It is true that we do have rules in our churches. But they should be based upon the Word of God. Rules are necessary to safeguard the testimony of the church. They also provide guidelines for conduct so that a Christian will not stray from his commitment to Jesus Christ.

You ask why the Bible cannot be the only rule we need. Many of our modern sins were unknown in Bible days. Ecclesiastes 7:29 says that "God hath made man upright; but they have sought out many inventions." And when these "inventions" are made, they are evil when they pull a person away from his uprightness.

In Bible times, they did not have such things as cigarettes, narcotics, motion pictures, television, professional sports, mini-skirts, and many other things that technology and modern lifestyles have given our generation. Since these things were invented after the Bible was written, we must have rules governing our conduct with respect to them.

Yet these rules should be based upon principles taught in the Word of God. For instance, we condemn the use of tobacco as sin, and therefore have a rule that none of our members can smoke, chew tobacco, or dip snuff. As we earlier mentioned, tobacco is not specifically mentioned in the Bible, for its use was unknown in those days. It was introduced to the "civilized" world by explorers who obtained it from the Indians of the New World.

Even though tobacco was unknown in Bible days and therefore not mentioned in Scripture, such passages as I Corinthians 3:17; I Corinthians 6:12, 19, 20; and II Corinthians 7:1 proclaim divine principles which condemn its use.

The application of biblical principles results in rules which are especially important for the young either in years or spiritual attainments. Although mature Christians should have their spiritual sensibilities keenly trained "to discern both good and evil" (Hebrews 5:14), it is sad to note that many do not, and therefore rules also help these saints to know how to conduct themselves in an ungodly social climate.

A person may chafe against rules, but if he is truly spiritual and consecrated he would not do so; he would realize that rules serve to assist the church in keeping a fellowship clean from compromise and contamination, and to help people be ready for the soon return of our Lord.

•••••••••••

Churches Differ on Standards

QUESTION:

The standard of holiness in dress and hair in our church is different than a neighboring church. My pastor is stricter than the other pastor, and insists that we obey him and the standard of holiness he preaches. I can't see why we have to be different from the other church. If they can dress differently and be saved, why can't we?

ANSWER:

I can understand your confusion. I hope the day will come when we all can speak with one voice on these matters and have a unified standard all over our fellowship. Frankly, however, it seems to me that the day is still far off when everyone sees eye-to-eye on every point.

But let us not magnify these differences. For the most part they are minor. We stand united on the major, important things relative to dress. We all believe in long, uncut hair for our girls and women, short, cut hair for boys and men. We believe in modest apparel for both sexes, the women's dresses covering their knees and upper arms with no sheers or "see-throughs" and no tight skirts, and the men with no tight pants, effeminate styles, or long hair.

Having said this, let me now stress the value of convictions, and the solid ground a pastor is on when he teaches and preaches additional convictions to his people, whether other ministers do or not.

God has little use for namby-pamby, spineless, follow-the-crowd weaklings, whether in the pulpit or in the pew. The men God has used have always been men of deep personal conviction. When a minister compromises his convictions for expediency's sake, because of threats that his saints will leave him unless he does, or to follow the lead of another minister who is getting a crowd, he is then in deep trouble.

First he loses his self-respect, knowing he has sold out. Then, even those worldly-minded members of his congregation who want to compromise lose respect for him, although they might have been the very ones that urged him to do so. The holiness-minded saints are bewildered and ashamed. Worst of all, his ministry loses its power and anointing. He becomes a hireling, and Satan has his number. The downhill slide never stops once the momentum has begun. "Ichabod," the glory has departed, is eventually written over the church door. I am sure you do not want this to happen. Therefore you should be glad that your pastor is a strong man, a man of conviction and spirituality.

Here is a verse of Scripture we should never forget: "Obey [that is, outwardly conform to your pastor's teaching in full obedience] them that have the rule over you [God has not given the neighboring pastor the oversight of your soul, but He has given it to your pastor], and submit yourselves [this is an inward attitude void of resentment or secret desires to disobey or rebel]: for they watch for your souls [your pastor is burdened for you, that you will be saved], as they that must give account [never forget that God will call your pastor to account for the conviction He has given him to preach], that they may do it with joy, and not with grief [a disobedient or rebellious saint is a grief to his pastor, and it will turn out to be a grief to that saint when the pastor gives account of his disobedience to God]: for that is unprofitable for you" (Hebrews 13:17).

Finally, suppose the neighboring pastor is wrong and your pastor is right? The chances are that the strictest one is closer to the will of God and God's true standard of holiness than the more lenient one. It is always safe to adhere to the strictest standard you can. Take it from God when your pastor preaches it—he does not do it because he enjoys it, but because he wants you to make it into heaven.

You are not responsible to obey the pastor of a neighboring church. But you are responsible to obey your own pastor. The old saying, "The grass is greener on the other side of the fence" is not always true. The blessing of God will come into your heart only when you stop looking across the fence, pray through, obey your pastor with gladness, and rejoice that your pastor is a man with deep and God-given convictions. By submitting to his leadership, you will make it through to heaven.

• • • • • • • • • • • •

Guidelines for Christian Dress

QUESTION:

Our styles of dress are so different today from Bible times, how can we really know how we should dress? Does the Bible give specific guidelines as to how a Christian should dress?

ANSWER:

There are six main lines of teaching in the Bible on the subject of Christian's dress. In brief they are:

(1) *Vanity.* God is concerned that we not be vain in our dress. The divine admonition is ". . .that women adorn themselves in modest apparel, with shamefacedness and sobriety; not with broided hair, or gold, or pearls, or costly array" (I Timothy 2:9).

Pride is a lie. It tries to make the flesh more than it is. Pride results in a two-fold curse: first, a person loses his spiritual perspective and fails to see his utter need to depend upon God for everything. Thus he begins to live to himself and, as a result, to cut himself off from God. Second, a person becomes self-righteous and is lifted up in his imagination beyond his true self.

Any clothing which vaunts the ego, whether jewels and plumes, snazzy jet-set styles, or hip-style hippie attire, is contrary to Scripture.

(2) *Confusing the sexes.* God is concerned that we do not dress so as to appear like the opposite sex. God reveals His feelings about this in Deuteronomy 22:5: "The woman shall not wear that which pertaineth unto a man, neither shall a man put on a woman's garment: for all that do so are abomination unto the LORD thy God."

Some argue that in Bible days both men and women wore long robes. While this fact is true, there were clear distinctions in styles that distinguished the dress of men from women. The scriptural injunction was made against a person crossing these distinctive styles to look like the opposite sex. They were not to try and become, appear, or feel like the opposite sex.

There are several reasons for this: first, it confuses the distinction God ordained between the sexes (not just physically, but emotionally). Moreover, unisex clothing can be a temptation for homosexuality which God hates and forbids. Lastly, it gives occasion for rape, adultery, and assault.

In Western societies, both men and women wear pants. It appears that one motive for women wearing pants is rebellion (often called "women's liberation"); they want to confuse the sexes in their efforts to "liberate" women from a male dominated society.

For a woman to wear pants or other masculine dress,

or for men to dress feminine is loathsome to God. Unisex dress is condemned in the Bible.

(3) *Immodesty.* God wants our bodies to be covered.

When God made man in the beginning, He covered him with the glory of God's shekinah (Psalm 8:5; *crowned:* literally "encircled or compassed about"). When sin came, Adam and Eve saw that they were naked (Genesis 3:7; literally "stripped"). God killed an innocent animal and clothed them with its skin (Genesis 3:21). His plan is for our bodies to be covered.

One of the signs of insanity and demon possession is that the victim wants to tear his clothes off. (See Luke 8:27.) Our generation manifests the diabolical influences at work in our society by the frenzied plunge to nudity being displayed everywhere. But when Jesus healed the naked demoniac, he immediately clothed himself (Luke 8:35).

Immodesty, particularly in women, kindles the lustful base nature in men by goading, teasing, enticing them to sin. In these cases, man may be guilty of sin, but the woman is not blameless. This is how David fell into sin (II Samuel 11:2). This must never be the case in God's church, where women (and men too) are commanded to dress in "modest apparel" (I Timothy 2:9).

(4) *Identifying with the ungodly.* God is concerned about our identification—about whether we are identified with His church, or whether our dress identifies us with the pagans and the ungodly. Isaiah 2-3 is devoted to dealing with Israel, which had taken on the ways of the Philistines and idolators "from the east," whose land was "full of idols" (Isaiah 2:6-8). Some women in Israel had adopted the dress and the ways of these heathen: "the

daughters of Zion are haughty, and walk with stretched forth necks and wanton eyes, walking and mincing as they go, and making a tinkling with their feet" (Isaiah 3:16). In the following verses the Lord specified the articles of dress which they copied from the heathen, and He pronounced His judgment upon them.

God does not want us identifying ourselves with the ungodly! This principle is largely lost by many. It is not whether a beard or a style of pants is bad, but who and what a beard or the style of pants identifies the wearer with. The old saying, "Birds of feather flock together," is applicable here. When the apostles were "let go, they went to their own company." Which company is our company? What company do we identify with, dress like, fit into: the ungodly, or God's church?

A hippie was once asked what he believed and stood for. Pointing to his beard, long hair, and weird dress, he said, "I wear my hair and beard this way and dress this way so that everybody will know where I stand—that I am against the war and against the establishment, that I am an anarchist and a revolutionary, that I am against the 'pigs,' that I am for pot and for freedom of sex. My dress, my beard, and my lifestyle ought to tell you that."

If a man does not want sheep to think him a wolf, he should not walk among the flock on hands and knees with a wolfskin on! The little maid told Peter, "Thy speech betrayeth thee." So does our dress. It betrays which crowd we want to be identified with. Any Christian who dresses to appear like a sinful group identifies with them, and is under the same condemnation Israel was under in Isaiah 3.

The Apostle Peter's Pentecostal message was not only Acts 2:38, but it also included, "Save yourselves from this untoward generation" (Acts 2:40). Is a person saving himself from this rebellious generation when he copies the worldly crowd and identifies with them? Where does our dress fit in best? Does our dress fit in with the company of godly, Spirit-filled saints, or with those who know not God?

Spirit-filled people dress according to Christian custom. (See I Corinthians 11:16.) We should ask, does our dress say, "I belong to this world"? Or does it say, "I am separate from the world; I belong to God. I am not ashamed of my company, the people of God"? Our dress identifies us with either the godly or the ungodly.

(5) *Costliness.* God is concerned that we do not waste money on our apparel. "Costly array" is condemned in I Timothy 2:9 just as immodesty is. This is the basic reason why "adornments" of gold, pearls, and other costly ornaments are condemned.

While this principle is akin to the first one (vanity), it has also a very important additional involvement.

We are stewards of all we possess. That is, God has entrusted us with what money and goods we have to use for His glory. We are not to consider these things ours to do with as we like. Rather, God says, "Every beast of the forest is mine, and the cattle upon a thousand hills. . .for the world is mine, and the fulness thereof" (Psalm 50:10, 12). "The silver is mine, and the gold is mine, saith the LORD of hosts" (Haggai 2:8).

To take our possessions which the Lord gave us and use them to buy costly ornaments to adorn our flesh is a gross misuse of our stewardship. They are entrusted to us to advance the kingdom of God, not to bring glory to our flesh. What right have we to "consume upon our own lusts" that which God has entrusted to us to use for His glory when a world of souls is dying that was so dearly purchased with the precious blood of Jesus?

(6) *Typology*. God is concerned that we do not violate the types (symbolical meanings) of Scripture.

To the unlearned in God's Word, symbolism may mean nothing, but the Bible makes it very clear that God is concerned that all types be exalted perfectly.

For example, when Moses violated the type by striking the rock twice instead of striking it once, God refused to permit him to enter the Promised Land. God had intended the incident to symbolize Christ, smitten once for all on Calvary, and who now is our High Priest to whom we submit our needs in prayer. But that type was broken by Moses, and Moses suffered his greatest loss.

The plain commandments in I Corinthians 11 that dealing with the hair of both men and women have to do with this principle. Man is a type of Christ; woman is a type of the church. Long hair is symbolical of subjection. For a man to have long hair is to symbolize that Christ is not the head of the church. For a woman to cut her hair is to teach (by typology) that the church need not be subject to Christ.

If to keep long hair is more important to a man than to have fellowship with Christ, his long hair becomes an idol—something that stands between God and man that is held in more esteem than God. Disobedience to the commands of I Corinthians 11 (or any command elsewhere) becomes idolatry. "For rebellion is as the sin of witchcraft, and stubbornness is as iniquity and idolatry" (I Samuel 15:23).

These six divine guiding principles keep us in the will of God and answer questions relative to our dress today just as they did in Bible times.

•••••••••••

Public Swimming

QUESTION:

I have strong convictions on mixed swimming at pools, lakes, beaches and creeks. However, there are some church people who believe it is all right for men and women, boys and girls to mix-swim in private with their church group as long as they swim with all their clothes on. Is there any Scripture you can give me for guidance in this matter?

ANSWER:

Perhaps I Timothy 2:9 is the verse of Scripture you desire.

Some years ago while returning from a radio broadcast with a group of our young people, one young lady asked me, "Pastor, what is wrong with swimming?"

I replied, "Nothing. It's good, healthful exercise."

Astonished, she responded, "Then why won't my father let me go swimming?"

I said, "Probably it is because of the garments you wear."

Immediately she understood and subsided with an audible "Oh!"

It should be obvious to all holiness-minded people that modern bathing suits are, to say the least, indecent. Except for completely private swimming involving only your immediate family, or swimming only with others of the same sex, these suits should never be worn.

Further, even though you may be dressed in clothing that is modest when dry, oftentimes such clothing may become quite revealing when wet, clinging to the body in a most immodest way. So one must be careful when bathing even when wearing clothing which fully covers the body.

Even when modesty of dress prevails, there is also the temptation when frolicking in the water for modest conventions which ordinarily prevail between sexes to break down. Care must be taken that this does not develop.

Perhaps it should be added that another consideration is the attire (or lack of it) of others in the bathing area. To mix with the near-nude crowd on the beaches today is unwise for a child of God, even though he may be properly dressed. It is a good rule to stay away from public bathing areas when other bathers are nearby.

Your pastor's wishes should always be the deciding factor as to whether or not it is permissible for mixed church groups to swim with all their clothes on in a private place if precautions concerning these things are kept in mind. He may feel that it is not wise under the circumstances. Always submit yourself to his guidance and authority in such matters.

One final observation. More and more over the past twenty years our beaches and other bathing spots have become the gathering areas for the lowest and most depraved characters of our modern society. In many beach areas unlawful acts of vandalism, debauchery, and licentiousness are openly practiced. People of refinement own- ing beach-front homes sell out in disgust because their front yards have been turned into latrines and garbage dumps. Orgies and wild saturnalias featuring open nudi- ty and fornication are commonplace occurrences. Pot smoking is openly practiced. Dope addicts pilfer, van- dalize, and steal. Many beaches are covered with garbage, and broken beer bottles strew the sands. I do not think these areas are fit for decent society, let alone true Christians.

Only one reason should take you to such an area: to witness of the saving power of Jesus and to glorify His name!

•••••••••••

Immodest Apparel

QUESTION:

Why does my pastor say that it is immodest to wear skirts that do not cover the knees? It might have been con- sidered immodest thirty years ago to wear skirts above the knees, but this is another age. Nobody thinks a thing about it today, and surely it does not rouse lustful thoughts in the boys because they see much more than that all the time. I think that skirts just above the knees are modest today, because many girls wear them much higher.

ANSWER:

One of the dangerous teachings of this modern day is "situation ethics" or "ethical relativism," meaning that there are no fixed standards or laws, that changing circumstances alter cases, and what was considered sin at one time need not necessarily be considered sin at another.

But God's Word stands forever! God has never changed His mind about what constitutes an adequate covering for the body, or what is modest and what is immodest. God wants our bodies to be covered in a way that He considers decent and modest.

Isaiah 47:2-3 reveals what God calls "nakedness" or immodesty. It is to "make bare the leg" and "uncover the thigh."

The minimum standard of modesty, it seems to me from this passage of Scripture, is for ladies to wear dresses that fully cover the knees at all times so that no part of their thighs are ever uncovered, even when they sit down.

This, I am convinced, is God's minimum standard of modesty which has never changed and never will change no matter what fads and fashions of dress, or undress, may come on the scene.

You may "kick against the pricks," but don't ever forget that if your heart is right you will obey your pastor gladly and cheerfully. Not only so, but you will have such a love for holiness and such an abhorrence of worldliness that you will allow God to set your standards as to whether a dress is modest or not, and not your ungodly or worldly-minded friends!

Watching Parades

QUESTION:

I realize that our pastors teach not to mix on public swimming beaches because the devil can be very tempting among a crowd of undressed people, but how come it seems to be all right to watch a parade of prancing, dancing, half-dressed girls? How do you feel about going to the parades of the world?

ANSWER:

Unquestionably we are living in a day when nudity and sex are blatantly and brazenly displayed. That which was at one time practiced only behind locked doors and drawn shades is now made a public spectacle. The days of immodesty are upon us!

We have taken a stand against participating with the world in the display of our bodies. Our *Articles of Faith* under the heading of "Holiness" states our position on this point:

> *"We wholeheartedly disapprove of our people indulging in any acitivities which are not conducive to good Christianity and godly living, such as theatres, dances, mixed bathing, women cutting their hair, make-up, any apparel that immodestly exposes the body, all worldly sports and amusements, and unwholesome radio programs and music. Furthermore, because of the display of all these evils on television, we disapprove of any of our people having television sets in their homes."*

146

And under the heading of "Public School Activities" the *Articles of Faith* states:

"We disapprove of school students attending shows, dances, dancing classes, theatres, engaging in school activities against their religious scruples, and wearing gymnasium clothes which immodestly expose the body."

Behind these two articles setting forth the regulations concerning our conduct lies the great scriptural principle of being "transformed by the renewing of your mind" (Romans 12:2). We refuse to join the crowd, to participate with them in immodestly exposing our bodies, because we now have a new mind, a mind that desires to be like Jesus.

While we refuse to indulge in the licentious display of our own bodies, there is simply no way in which we can regulate what the world does. The world all about us flaunts their disregard for decency in their mad, sinful dash toward hell. And whether we desire to witness the ungodly scenes all around us or not, we are forced to view them at times, and so are our children. And it is not God's will for us to become hermits. We must remain *in* the world while not being *of* it. We should use all means at our disposal with the help of the Holy Ghost to guide and train our children to think holy, talk holy, act holy, and "be not conformed to this world." This includes using your good common sense.

The key is to be filled with the Holy Ghost and have our minds renewed. We will then "abhor that which is evil, cleave to that which is good" (Romans 12:9). With the Holy Ghost in control we will not look on a woman

147

to lust after her, which Jesus said is committing adultery with her already in the heart (Matthew 5:28).

While there are many spectacles that are worthwhile viewing, a child of God must not knowingly or deliberately throw himself open to view a licentious display which could result in lustful desire. If the parades to which you refer are of this nature, by all means refrain.

Wearing Clothes of the Opposite Sex

QUESTION:

At camp meeting I heard the teaching that the Mosaic Law is put away. Reference was made that we no longer observe the law in regard to sowing diverse seeds, wearing two types of materials, or eating a ham sandwich. Since we do not observe Deuteronomy 22:9-11, does this mean that Deuteronomy 22:5 is also done away with?

ANSWER:

I appreciate your concern inasmuch as Deuteronomy 22:5 speaks of a very important principle:

> *"The woman shall not wear that which pertaineth unto a man, neither shall a man put on a woman's garment: for all that do so are abomination unto the LORD thy God" (Deuteronomy 22:5).*

The key to understanding whether or not this verse

is to be observed today is found in the last words of the
verse: "all that do so are abomination unto the LORD thy
God." Farrar Fenton translates this phrase, "God abhors
all who do this." *The New International Version* says they
are doing something "detestable" to God. *Strong's Exhaustive Concordance* says the meaning of the Hebrew
word is "something disgusting, i.e. an abhorrence." We
cannot get much stronger than that to express God's
loathing of those who wear the clothing of the opposite
sex.

The verses dealing with mixing seeds and garments
(Deuteronomy 22:9-11) do not indicate any such thought.
Although there were prohibitions expressed relative to
these matters, there is no thought of repugnance on the
part of God, no mention that these were an abomination
to God. The purpose of the prohibition against mixing
seeds and kinds of cloth was for an entirely different
reason. These commandments were given to the people
of Israel solely as a reminder that they were a separate
people unto God and were not to mix with the heathen
nations. (See Leviticus 20:24-26.) God used the most common everyday customs and activities of their lives to constantly remind them. They were to remember the fruit
of their land belonged to God every time they planted the
soil (verse 9); they were reminded the land was the Lord's
every time they plowed it (verse 10); and they were
reminded that they themselves belonged to God and Him
alone every morning when they put on their clothes (verse
11).

God did not "detest" or "abhor" mixed seed and
mixed kinds of clothing, nor were they "disgusting" or
an "abhorrence" unto Him. He did not say those things

were an abomination unto Him. It was simply that these commands were given to Israel as a reminder that they were to maintain their separation unto God.

When we receive the Holy Ghost, we do not need that kind of a reminder. "The Spirit itself beareth witness with our spirit, that we are the children of God" (Romans 8:16). These outward reminders were done away with when the law was nailed to the cross of Christ. (See Colossians 2:14-17.) Now we have the substance of which these things were merely types and shadows.

In Deuteronomy 22:5 a totally different kind of statement is made. In this verse the wearing of the apparel of the opposite sex is called "an abomination unto the LORD." This means that God *detests* women who wear men's clothes and men who wear women's clothes; to God it is disgusting, and He "abhors all who do this." This verse was not a type of something to come, nor was it a reminder of something else to Israel. Rather, it is a revelation of God's heart, of His feelings, of His righteous nature, of that which is a terrible sin in His eyes, and *He does not change!* Even though the law was done away with in Christ, the things that God abhorred, detested, and hated during the time of the law, He still abhors, detests, and hates today! "I am the LORD, I change not" (Malachi 3:6).

Dispensations may change, administrations change, covenants change, but God does not change. He feels exactly about things as He always has. With Him there is "no variableness, neither shadow of turning" (James 1:17). If ever He felt a certain way about something, you can be sure He still feels that way about it!

Wherever you find these words, "an abomination unto

the LORD," you may just settle it that God hates it, has always hated it, and will never cease to hate it. It is loathsome, disgusting, abhorrent, and abominable, and all who are abominable will be cast into the lake of fire (Revelation 21:8)!

············

Homosexuality

QUESTION:

The office of the General Assembly of the United Presbyterian Church takes the view that homosexuals are no less a part of the family of God than anyone else and that evidences of the grace of God and the call of the ministry have been found among their number. (See the February 1978 issue of **The Magazine for the United Presbyterian Family**.*) Would you please comment on this.*

ANSWER:

It is incredible, absolutely unbelievable to me that anyone in his right mind could tolerate homosexuality or look upon it as acceptable among those who claim to be the followers of Jesus.

The name Christian means Christlike, or one who belongs to Christ. Jesus was God manifest in the flesh (I Timothy 3:16), and was "holy, harmless, undefiled, separate from sinners" (Hebrews 7:26). In both Old and New Testaments this holy God expressed His divine displeasure and wrath against homosexuality (Leviticus

18:22; 20:13; Romans 1:24-28). Whenever the subject of homosexuality is dealt with in Scripture, it is depicted as a loathsome, degraded, perverted way of life that leads certainly to eternal damnation.

The marvel of true Christianity is that it does not leave the sinner in his sins, but saves him *from* his sins (I Corinthians 6:11 and Romans 6:1-7). In I Corinthians 6:9-10, homosexuality is included among the sins that will bar heaven's door against the one who indulges in that sin. But then verse 11 follows by declaring that "such were some of you: but ye are washed, but ye are sanctified, but ye are justified in the name of the Lord Jesus, and by the Spirit of our God." Salvation delivers sinners, including homosexuals, and they no longer engage in such sins. Hallelujah!

II Corinthians 5:17 declares that a saved person is a changed person, actually a new creation: "If any man be in Christ, he is a new creature: old things are passed away; behold, all things are become new." If a homosexual is genuinely saved, he will cease to be homosexual, just as a fornicator or adulterer will cease to be engaged in their form of sinning. A homosexual will be delivered, changed, set free, and made a new creature. To say one can be both a Christian and a homosexual is a contradiction in terms. It is impossible.

Our word *sodomy* came into the language as a description of the homosexuality that was rampant in ancient Sodom. When God wanted to picture sin at its grossest and most brazen, He pointed to Sodom.

There is also a spirit of Sodom. Sodom wanted its rights. The attitude of the men of Sodom was that each should be allowed to do what he wanted to do when he wanted to do it. The spirit of the homosexual is, "Nobody has any right to tell me what I can do or what I can't do." This lustful, devilish spirit sometimes gets into the church. One with that spirit will say, "The pastor has no right to tell me how to dress, how to talk, or walk, or act. I'm just going to do as I please. I have the Holy Ghost just like he has." God hates this spirit. It is the spirit of the homosexual. It is from the pit, and it will return to the pit.

As your question indicates, homosexuality has insinuated itself right into professing Christendom, even among the clergy. It is as Antichrist sitting in the temple of God.

Recently a tract by David Wilkerson was sent me by one of our ministers. Mr. Wilkerson is concerned about what is happening in the charismatic revival. While not Oneness, David Wilkerson is to be commended for his forthright stand against the infiltration of homosexuality. The following is a quotation from his tract:

Jesus hates homosexuality, but He loves homosexuals. He forgives those who repent and forsake their evil ways. But now the [professing] church has within its ranks those who would have us believe Jesus no longer considers homosexuality a sin.

Homosexuals now claim more than 50,000 members in their "all-homosexual" churches. The Metropolitan Community Church is one of the many homosexual denominations springing up across the nation. I sent an observer to one of their "Holy Ghost" conventions in Dallas, Texas. What unbelievable blasphemy!

Each delegate, as they registered, was given a packet which included, among other things, two "boy" magazines

*of all nude men and a list of all the gay bars in Dallas—
so that delegates could leave the evening service, go to their
selected bar, and connect with a lover for the night. And,
those delegates called themselves "ministers!"*

*How they did sing! They praised the Lord with en-
thusiasm; but their evangelist corrupted the gospel beyond
comprehension. He said, "Sure, Paul condemned men who
changed the natural use and burned one toward another.
But that's not us. We were born this way. So, come out
of your closets. Be filled with the Holy Ghost, and enjoy
your homosexuality."*

*How long will Jesus put up with this outrageous blas-
phemy? How long will our blessed Lord permit "ministers" of the church to excuse and encourage homosexuals
in their perversion? . . .Jesus is not coming back for a
church that pampers and excuses sin. So, beware! Beware
of ministers who excuse vile sin with the whitewash of what
they call Christian "love." You cannot bring healing to
homosexuals by sympathizing with their sin. Beware of
those who come in the name of Jesus who refuse to see the
exceeding sinfulness of this sin.*

I can say a hearty "amen" to those words of David
Wilkerson. I conclude with another excerpt from the same
tract, with some additional words inserted in the last
sentence.

*Our children face an age when it will seem like every
demon in hell has been set loose to deceive. They will face
seductions no other generation has heard of. Satan will
assault them with every device at his disposal. Evil men*

154

will wax worse and worse. Crime and violence will threaten their very lives. "Gay goons" will stalk the streets of cities, raping men and killing, as they did in the days of Lot. The stench of hell will be almost everywhere.

But Jesus has promised the last-day believer more grace than all other generations. Satan doesn't know it, but all his attacks will do nothing but help produce a kind of "super saint." Jesus will raise up, in the midst of madness and despair, a holy seed. [Strong, separated, and unbending young men and women, baptized in Jesus' name, filled with the Holy Ghost, will withstand and overcome Satan through the power of Jesus' name!]

•••••••••••

"Doesn't God Love the 'Gays'?"

QUESTION:

I really don't see why a gay person is discriminated against, and why he cannot be saved. If God made him that way, how can he help it? Doesn't God love the gays too?

ANSWER:

In the first place, a "gay" person is not gay. He is miserable, for he is not the person God intended him to be. God did not make anyone homosexual. We are told in Genesis 1:27 that "God created man in his own image, in the image of God created he him; male and female created he them." The reason that God made them male and female was that they might "be fruitful and multiply and replenish the earth" (verse 28). The practice of homosexuality completely nullifies the plan of God, for homosexuals cannot reproduce. Therefore, to be "that way" is a product of the devil and a hideous abnormality.

Since they cannot reproduce they must recruit. Homosexuals are not content to have relations only with their usual companions. They must continually conquer new territory and enlist new converts to their perversions. Thus a recent "gay" publication gave detailed instructions how to seduce pre-teen boys, and stated that their goal is to recruit new converts to the practice of their unnatural vice so that by the year 2000 one-half of the population of the United States will be homosexual.

It is our young children and youth that must be protected from these monsters.

The Bible in two instances relates occasions when homosexuals endeavored to seduce and recruit others and force them to submit to this hellish and evil practice (Genesis 19:1-13; Judges 19:22-24).

God was so anxious to protect Israel from the damning influence of homosexuality that He pronounced it an abomination and made it punishable by death (Leviticus 18:22; 20:13). He destroyed the entire cities of Sodom and Gomorrah because they practiced this vice (Jude 7).

Asa was one of the good kings of Judah. Among his other good deeds, he was commended in Scripture for removing the sodomites from the land (I Kings 15:11, 12).

In I Corinthians 6:9-10 the words *effeminate* and *abusers of themselves with mankind* could better be translated "homosexual perverts" as in *Today's English Version.* And In these verses God says twice that they "shall not inherit the kingdom of God."

Near the end of the New Testament we read of the beauties of heaven. Then it says in Revelation 22:15 that "without are dogs, and sorcerers, and whoremongers, and murderers, and idolators, and whosoever loveth and maketh a lie." These are forever excluded from God's presence. The term *dogs* is shown by Deuteronomy 23:17-18 to mean "male prostitutes, sodomites" *(NASV)*. In those days dogs were not the family pets they are today. The term was one of loathing and contempt.

You ask if God loves the "gays." Of course He does. He loves all sinners. He loves them too much to permit them to continue in their vile perversions and still be saved. He provided a salvation that delivers and changes them.

In the verses we previously quoted (I Corinthians 6:9-10) which states that homosexuals shall not enter heaven, Paul reminded the Corinthians that before their conversion some of them had been in homosexuality among other sins. Then he added, "But ye are washed, but ye are sanctified, but ye are justified in the name of the Lord Jesus, and by the Spirit of our God." So a homosexual can be saved and delivered if he genuinely repents of his sin, is baptized in Jesus' name for the remission of sins, receives the Holy Ghost, and lives a victorious, overcoming life in the Spirit (Galatians 6:16).

The whole matter hinges on the individual's desire. If he justifies his sin and is content to live in his perversion, he can receive no help from God. But when he recognizes the satanic origin of his problem and cries for

157

salvation through the blood of Jesus, he can be delivered by obeying the gospel. But his repentance must be deep enough so that he will never indulge in this abominable act of homosexual relations again.

Why Are Homosexuals That Way?

QUESTION:

I am writing this letter with reference to homosexuality and bisexuality. My father is bisexual and my mother is homosexual, and a few years later my sister became homosexual. My question is: Why are homosexuals and bisexuals the way they are?

ANSWER:

Before we answer your question, it is important that we know the meaning of the terms you use in your letter. An individual who is homosexual is attracted only to persons of his or her own sex, while a bisexual individual is equally attracted to both sexes, to both male and female persons. For convenience sake, however, since both are attracted to members of their own sex, both may be termed homosexual.

Homosexuality is not normal; this condition is not the way God planned for humans to be. God did not make a man or a woman this way. In the beginning God made Adam of the dust of the ground. Then God said, "It is not good that the man should be alone; I will make him an help meet for him" (Genesis 2:18). God caused Adam to sleep and removed a rib from his side. The passage tells us:

> *"And the rib, which the LORD God had taken from man, made he a woman, and brought her unto the man. And Adam said, This is now bone of my bones, and flesh of my flesh: she shall be called Woman, because she was taken out of Man. Therefore shall a man leave his father and his mother, and shall cleave unto his wife: and they shall be one flesh" (Genesis 2:22-24).*

God did not make another man out of the rib and present that man to Adam to be his companion. God never made a homosexual or a bisexual man or woman. That came about through sin. Satan is the author of homosexuality!

Contrary to all the humanistic and anti-Christian propaganda with which we are being deluged today, and in spite of all that ungodly psychologists and psychiatrists say, no one is ever born a homosexual. Oh, I know that every individual is born with all the possibilities to commit any and every sin in Satan's catalog. But no man is born in such a condition that he can say, "I was born to this abnormal and sinful lifestyle, and I cannot help it. I am destined and fated for this kind of life. Therefore this is normal and right for me." That is a lie. Homosexuals and bisexuals are made, not born the way they are. The question might rightly be asked, "Then how did these individuals become homosexual and bisexual?"

If you will carefully read Romans 1:18-32, you will find that homosexuality is a curse from God because of an individual's rejection of God. Verses 26-27 plainly declare that it is "for this cause [that] God gave them up unto vile affections," and then describe the homosexuality of both women and men. Verse 28 continues and says this has happened because "they did not like to retain God in their knowledge"; therefore "God gave them over to a reprobate mind to do those things which are not convenient (to perform unmentionable deeds—*Phillips*)."

Of course, it is also possible that parents who are themselves reprobates and homosexual will bring up their children in an atmosphere charged with evil and corruption, and that the child will take on the homosexuality of the parents. It is also possible that the child may be subjected to an abnormal and unscriptural reversal of roles of father and mother, with the mother dominant and the father effeminate. This may cause confusion in the child as to the sexes and resultant twisting of sexual attitudes. It may be that this is the case in your family, where your sister became homosexual under the influence of a homosexual father and mother. May I urge you to keep yourself pure and filled with the Holy Ghost and God will keep you from this evil.

Be assured of this: homosexuality is never condoned in Scripture. It is condemned everywhere in God's Word. In fact, God sent fire and brimstone upon Sodom because of this sin; and from this came the word *sodomy*, the term for the filthy homosexual act. The Bible terms homosexuals "dogs" because of their base and corrupt nature. (See Deuteronomy 23:17-18.) In Revelation 22:15 "dogs" (homosexuals) are classified with sorcerers, whoremongers, murderers, and idolators, and are forever barred from heaven.

Three godly kings of Judah, Asa, Jehoshaphat, and Josiah were blessed by God for driving the sodomites out of the land (I Kings 15:12; 22:46; II Kings 23:7).

This does not mean that we should hate homosexuals. We should love all men, but hate their sin. Jude speaks of the soulwinner snatching souls out of their filth and the fire of their burning, "hating even the garment spotted by the flesh" (Jude 23). So we should have a loving concern for homosexuals, but let them know that our love is not a condoning of their sin; to the contrary, it is a concern for them to abandon their abnormal manner of living, for there is no salvation for homosexuals who continue in their sin.

Is there hope for homosexuals? Yes, but only if they forsake their sin and turn to God with all their heart and with all their soul. They will never get help and will never be saved through halfway measures. The only hope of a homosexual individual is a genuine new birth experience of water and Spirit, and then a life of prayer and consecration to God. I Corinthians 6:9-11 includes homosexuals ("effeminate, abusers of themselves with mankind") who have been washed, sanctified, and justified "in the name of the Lord Jesus and by the Spirit of our God." And the same power that saved them from that awful sin can also keep them from returning to it again, as a "dog. . .to his own vomit" (II Peter 2:22).

•••••••••••

Abortion

QUESTION:

Is it wrong to have an abortion if the baby would be unwanted because it is the result of sin? Especially since I am a teen-age girl who cannot support or take care of the child?

ANSWER:

Sin always reaps a painful reward. To try to circumvent its penalty by committing another sin is wickedness. The old saying is true: "Two wrongs do not make one right."

Make no mistake, abortion is murder! God will see to it that a fearful toll will be taken upon the one who commits such a deed, both in the mind, in the body, and in the soul. The only mitigating factor in such a case would be to save the life of the mother.

The Bible is plain concerning this matter:

1. The fruit of the womb belongs to God. "Lo, children are an heritage of the LORD: and the fruit of the womb is his reward" (Psalm 127:3).
2. God forms the child in the womb. "As thou knowest not what is the way of the spirit, nor how the bones do grow in the womb of her that is with child: even so thou knowest not the works of God who maketh all" (Ecclesiastes 11:5). "Did not he that made me in the womb make him? and did not one fashion us in the womb?" (Job 31:15).
3. It is God that takes the child out of the womb. "But thou art he that took me out of the womb. . ." (Psalm

22:9). "By thee have I been holden up from the womb.
thou art he that took me out of my mother's bowels:
my praise shall be continually of thee" (Psalm 71:6).
Thus only God has the right to take children from the
womb ahead of time.

4. God considers the unborn, undeveloped child in the
womb as though it were fully formed. "For thou hast
possessed my reins: thou hast covered me in my
mother's womb. I will praise thee; for I am fearfully
and wonderfully made: marvelous are thy works; and
that my soul knoweth right well. My substance was
not hid from thee, when I was made in secret, and
curiously wrought in the lowest parts of the earth.
Thine eyes did see my substance, yet being unperfect;
and in thy book all my members were written, which
in continuance were fashioned, when as yet there was
none of them" (Psalm 139:13-16).

5. Miscarriage is a curse. "Give them, O LORD: what wilt
thou give? give them a miscarrying womb and dry
breasts" (Hosea 9:14). Verse 13 says this curse is
"bringing forth his children to the murderer."

6. Man-induced abortion was not permitted to go un-
punished, even when it was an accident. (See Exodus
21:22-25.)

You may argue that the Supreme Court of the United
States has declared that the fetus in the womb is not a
human being until after the third month, but God declares
otherwise!

Many a woman is haunted day and night with horrible guilt, knowing she will some day face God with blood
on her hands, the blood of her own unborn child.

To my dying day I will never forget the tormented

wail of a woman calling me on the telephone at 4:00 in the morning. Over fifty years old, she had lived as a saint in a Pentecostal church for years, but now having suffered a heart attack, her tortured soul must bare its guilty secret. She had had an abortion, and had lived with her guilt for many years, but knew she could not meet God with this terrible sin on her conscience. She said, "Oh Brother Gray, if you only knew how I have lived for years with this horrible darkness. Even in church when others get blessed, the terrible blackness of my sin envelops me. I have never had a moment's peace." I am happy to say I was able to help her make her peace with God.

But suppose the heart attack had taken her? Perhaps you can excuse abortion, but I verily believe it is an act of murder. And some day the memory of your sin will rise up in your soul to torment you.

May I close by saying tht God will forgive your sin of fornication. But do not add sin to sin. I realize you will suffer shame as an unwed mother. But if you seek God He will forgive you. If you cannot keep your baby, there are many, many fine Christian people that would consider a baby to adopt and raise as a gift from heaven. Your baby would be loved, cared for, and grow up in a Christian home, and you would never regret your unselfish gift of love.

If you will do this, instead of sin and guilt haunting you, you will be able to rejoice that even though you have sinned, God has forgiven you, and you do not have to meet God with the blood of your unborn child on your hands.

•••••••••••

164

When Does an Infant Receive its Soul?

QUESTION:

When does a being (person) receive a soul? Is it during pregnancy or when a baby takes its first breath?

ANSWER:

We have a clue given to us in the record of man's creation. Genesis 2:7 says, "And the LORD God formed man of the dust of the ground, and breathed into his nostrils the breath of life; and man became a living soul."

The instant life was placed into that body, he became a living soul. The beginning of life and the entrance of the soul take place simultaneously. Therefore it is reasonable to assume that when the fetus in the womb has a heartbeat and life of its own it is at that point a living soul.

Abortion is a horrible act and sin against God whenever it is done. But abortion after life begins is doubly a sin because it is the destruction of a soul. Our nation will pay a fearful price for ignoring the warnings and plain teachings of Scripture in legalizing abortion. We cannot escape the awful consequences of our sinning against God.

•••••••••••

Rock Music and Worship

QUESTION:

It seems a big change in Pentecost today is the music. I am quite mixed up. I feel so guilty listening to some of the special songs because the music is like I used to dance to. I was taught not to listen to worldly music, not even to tap my foot to it. Now the people in the church clap their hands so loud that it is difficult to hear the words of the song—it is just the beat. I feel so condemned when in a service like that. I feel grieved inside. Yet other people are dancing, shouting, and seemingly getting blessed. Is there something wrong with me? I have the Holy Ghost and want with all my heart to please God.

ANSWER:

I love singing and music. It plays a vital part in true spiritual worship. Three types of songs are referred to in Ephesians 5:18, 19 and Colossians 3:16.

First there is the hymn or prayer-song, such as "Draw Me Nearer" or "Have Thine Own Way, Lord." Then there is the psalm or praise-song. A good example is "All Hail the Power of Jesus Name." Finally we have spiritual songs, songs about spiritual things, or gospel songs. These are testimony-songs such as "Since Jesus Came Into My Heart" and "When We All Get to Heaven."

While gospel songs are sung lively and joyfully with the whole congregation participating with rhythm and hand-clapping, it is certainly inappropriate for hymns or psalms to be sung in the same fashion. For instance, it could be sacrilegious to clap for songs that inspire solemnity and awe.

It is in the realm of lively gospel songs that this question relates.

I take the liberty to quote a recent issue of the *Sentinel,* the Texas District paper, under the heading "Rock Music in Church?" "The invasion is on! Public demand for rock music in the church is growing. Recently a large sign invited the public to attend the Gospel Rock Concert, Sunday at eleven o'clock.

"The youth music division of Singspiration, Inc. is called the Now Sounds! Our own churches are being invaded by the beat of the Beast and the twist of the Tempter!

"This attempt to pervert the music of our churches is effective because it comes disguised as an introduction to the 'Christian's view of the Arts.'

"Many gospel recording artists have accepted this form of music and singing as the best expression of their message to a lost world.

"Many choirs lack the depth of the singing of yesteryear, and they are replacing the glorious singing of the songs of Zion with the new beat, afterbeat, and demonic rhythm unrelated to the physical shout we have all enjoyed as a result of a spiritual experience.

"A gospel song with a fast tempo, with clapping of the hands and dancing in the Spirit is ever in order. But rock music inside the house of God, or anywhere else for that matter, is sinful.

"So let's face it. Born as we have been amid the great wealth of gospel music, augmented by the composition of Spirit-filled artists of our day, we should never be tempted to go out of the sphere of Christian harmony to seek unconsecrated sounds. It is absurd for a millionaire to steal!"

Well said! And now may I add a few observations.

I have just recently talked with a number of our older, seasoned ministers about the music now being heard in many of the churches and on albums put out by some Pentecostal singers. Many of these deeply spiritual warriors of the cross are troubled over the invasion of our Pentecostal ranks by the worldly type of music and singing. One of the mighty champions of Pentecost, a man whose spiritual stature is that of a giant, called me late one night so troubled that he could not sleep.

The infiltration of the worldly type of music is so subtle that the ungodly jungle beat is almost an accepted thing today. But godly men are alarmed.

Those who have made a study of modern music warn us that much of it is taken from devil-worshipers in Africa who use it to bring demon spirits down into their midst. The beat is hypnotic and sensual. Adding Christian words to it does not mitigate its insidious threat to either sanity or true spiritual worship.

Many times, even in churches, the beat is more important than the words. In fact, clapping is often so loud and overwhelming that neither the tune nor the words are discernable, only the beat.

I sympathize with your feelings. I too have gone home grieved in spirit and ashamed.

The singers sometimes urge the people to worship God, only to launch into the overwhelming tom-tom rhythm in which the people are caught away into the same frenzy as the devil worshipers, only in the name of the Holy One of Israel. An imposter has marched in, and the people are too gullible to be aware of what is happening! The flesh has taken over in the guise of "worship"! The people sway, clap, run, dance to the rhythm and the good feeling the flesh feels when it is moved upon by the beat, beat, beat of the overwhelming assault upon the basic human emotions, just like a rock festival!

If you think I am mistaken, pray for me. But our spiritual fathers would not tolerate what we are encouraging, not for one moment!

This was brought forcibly to my attention recently. At a "sacred concert" in one church a neighboring pastor brought a couple to whom he had been witnessing. They sat in the front, in the second row of seats. They were living together in an unmarried state. As the singing group went from one song to another, the beat increased. Emotions were stirred higher and higher. I noticed the young lady was clapping her hands over her head, swaying wildly from side to side with a look of ecstasy on her face. Then she started turning her head toward the young man every time she swayed against him. The next thing I knew she was kissing her paramour on every beat as she swayed with her hands up over her head.

Was she worshiping God? Far from it! She was carried away with the beat of the "Christian" songs into a public display of lustfulness. She was not being drawn to God, to conviction of her sins, or to a consciousness of her need of God. Rather it was the reverse. The music brought out her animal nature, and she was even more involved in the uncleanness of the fleshly realm in which she lived. All this through the music in one church service!

The Bible pattern is for our services to be such that when an unbeliever comes into our midst "the secrets of his heart [will be] made manifest; and so falling down on his face he will worship God, and report that God is in you of a truth" (I Corinthians 14:25). If our singing and music does not contribute to this end, something is wrong with it.

Why should we copy the ungodly? God has warned us to "learn not the way of the heathen" (Jeremiah 10:2).

Our churches must not be turned into rock festivals!

Let us rejoice in the Lord, but let us never confuse true worship with the music of the golden calf!

••••••••••••

Worldly Music in Church

QUESTION:

The issue is music; there seems to be different styles of gospel music. Some people enjoy a certain type or style of music and criticize the styles they don't like. Some people say, "Well, it's for God, it's praising God, so it's not for us to judge or criticize." Others have taken a strong stand from the pulpit and have said certain styles of music just should not be in the church, that the music is "worldly." Who is correct and how can I make sure scripturally?

ANSWER:

There is tremendous power in music. There are types of music by which individuals can be manipulated. Those who are knowledgable can use them to induce desired responses or release inhibitions. People can be actually "drugged" by this type of music until they lose control of themselves. Through clever use of music by unscrupulous manipulators, girls have lost their virtue, and boys ensnared in sodomy. Under its influence clothes are torn off and unlimited license prevails.

Certain types of music are used in devil worship and in seances. Another style is used in connection with the eastern religions from India. These induce trance-like

170

states which these religions feature. In both of those styles demons are present which lead the practitioners into awful darkness and eventual demon possession. This music is sweeping America today. Both "rock" music and much "contemporary" music are of satanic origin.

Because of greed some promoters have entered the gospel music field with these styles of music, simply substituting Christian words for non—Christian. It is a money-making proposition, pure and simple. Gullible Christians follow the lead of the ungodly. Foolishly, the church oftentimes, while not immediately adopting the styles of the world, follows the trend set by the world so it will not be looked upon by worldly-minded people as a back number and hopelessly old fashioned. The only difference is that it is six months to a year behind, but following nevertheless in the way the world is going.

I believe this type of compromise with the world is one of the earmarks of the endtime Laodicean church (Revelation 3:14-19), which is lukewarm and will be spewed out of God's mouth. On the other hand, the church of Philadelphia (Revelation 3:7-11), which will be ready for the Rapture, simply will not follow the worldly lead, but will hold to the pure, separate, clean standards of holiness without compromise unto the end.

It is "strange fire" indeed to try to worship God by means of music which brings demon spirits into operation and which unleashes the lower bodily passions. The saying I heard as a boy, "All tunes belong to God except the spittoon," is simply not true. It is the height of folly to take unholy music and present it to the Lord. I have never seen "contemporary" music bring the power down in a service, nor a "rock" song bring conviction to a sin-

171

ner. God does not operate in that atmosphere.

But when people sing the good old gospel songs and hymns, clap their hands unto the Lord, or raise them in genuine worship, that which is felt by saint and sinner alike is truly the Spirit of God and not some other spirit.

We are rich with wonderful gospel music. Why borrow tainted, polluted music, which is far inferior, from the world? Why should a millionaire want to borrow a counterfeit dollar?

Let us offer a pure sacrifice unto the Lord "as a sweet smelling savour" (Ephesians 5:2), not "strange fire" (Leviticus 10:1, 2), which brought the wrath of God, nor an offering to the Lord like that of Cain (Genesis 4:3-5; Jude 11-12).

I am sure there are those who feel that the addition of Christian words sanctifies the corrupt music and makes it acceptable to the Lord. To these I would say that the addition of pure spring water to sewage does not purify the filthy sewer water and make it fit to drink. Remember the first sin—the one that plunged the whole human race into depravity and despair? Today, as then, Satan is a past master of getting people to eat of the tree of (a mixture of) good and evil!

• • • • • • • • • • • •

Music With a Beat

QUESTION:

My daughter says that our church is inconsistent because it objects to Christian rock songs, while at the same time we use a strong beat and handclapping to such songs as *"Everybody will be happy over there." She loves rock-and-roll music and justifies it by accusing us of being inconsistent and hypocritical. I do not feel right about rock-style Christian music, but don't know how to answer her. Can you help me?*

ANSWER:

There is a great gulf fixed between such songs as "Everybody will be happy over there" and rock-and-roll. They are vastly different. I am sure your daughter knows that, even though she may say that we are inconsistent and hypocritical to justify her desire for so-called "Christian" rock songs. Let me explain briefly about the type of music called rock-and-roll: first by referring to something that happened a few years ago.

An attorney was defending a pornographic book before the Supreme Court of the United States. The essence of his remarks were that it would be hypocritical to bar this book so long as we permitted the public to have free access to the Bible (and he read certain portions of it) and some of the classics. His argument continued that since we permitted the Bible and these classical works to remain uncensored that to be consistent we must also permit this obscene book. Tragically, if I remember right, the Supreme Court agreed, and the flood gates were open for the filth and pornography to corrupt the minds of the people of the United States. Today there is no limit to the depths of depravity permitted in our society because of the spurious argument of that attorney and others like him.

I do not believe it is hypocritical to accept the Bible and at the same time to bar pornography. And I do not believe it is hypocritical to have convictions about certain types of music. I believe rock-and-roll is the pornography of music. It is demonic. It unleashes fleshly passions. It works upon the nervous system of individuals, producing disorientation and the breaking down of restraints. It causes young people to go into a riotous, uninhibited, lustful frenzy. It is hand-in-glove with the drug culture, with the occult and devil worship. It stimulates everything that is base, and impure, and ungodly. These are facts which have been documented and are available in libraries to any person if they would care to investigate. Many people close their eyes to these things just as cigarette smokers refuse to look into documented research concerning the effects of tobacco on an individual. Nevertheless, the facts remain.

Putting Christian words to obscene music does not purify the music. "Jesus rock" is as evil as other rock music. Oftentimes the heavy beat, repetition, and broken rhythm is so hypnotic that the words are not even heard or considered—just the drug-like effect of the beat upon the nervous system of the individual. It gives a "high"just like amphetamines or other drugs. And the words about Jesus or the gospel that might be sung along with the music has nothing to do with it. The feeling comes, not through devotion and love for Jesus, not through consecration, but purely and simply through fleshly reaction to the rock-and-roll beat exactly the same as if the words were "Baby, Baby, Baby, dim out all the lights!" Of course many young people like that music, for they do not have the spiritual maturity to understand the difference. We should help them.

It is in no way inconsistent to shout and clap hands

to the strong, solid rhythm of "Everybody will be happy over there," while at the same time take a firm, positive stand against the insidious and devilish snare of rock-and-roll. May our blessed Lord give you, along with all our parents and pastors, divine wisdom in helping our young people in this vital area.

●●●●●●●●●●●●

"Does it Make Any Difference to God About My Hair or the Way I Dress?"

QUESTION:

Why should how I wear my hair make any difference to God? Why should it make any difference to Him whether my hair is cut or not, whether it is short or long, whether I look masculine, or whether I look feminine? Why should it make any difference? Why should He be concerned with what I wear? All He is concerned about is my heart. Isn't that really the truth?

ANSWER:

The Bible (which is God's words to us right out of His heart) tells us that God does care, and that there are several sound and solid reasons why it does make a difference to Him. If we love God, we will want to listen to what He has to say, and then do those things that please Him and avoid doing those things that displease Him.

True, He is primarily concerned about your heart. But if your heart is as it ought to be, you will want to obey what He tells you to do in the words of the Book He has

175

given to us.

His Word says that it is disgraceful in God's eyes for a man to have long hair (I Corinthians 11:14).

His Word says that God has given long hair to a woman for a covering and a glory (I Corinthians 11:15).

His Word says that a woman must not pray or speak in church without her head being covered (I Corinthians 11:5) with long hair (verse 15).

His Word says that a man must not pray or speak in church unless the covering (of long hair) has been cut off (I Corinthians 11:4).

His Words says that God's churches have no custom contrary to this teaching (I Corinthians 11:16).

Why did God make these rules about hair? The study of typology explains this. Man is a type of Christ, woman of the church. Long hair is symbolical of subjection. For a man to have long hair is to symbolize that Christ is not the head of the church. For women to cut their hair is to teach that the church need not be subject to Christ. So you can see that God considers this a very important matter.

If we are real Christians, not just lukewarm, professing church members, we will respect God's express desires in this matter and want to please Him in every way.

Boys will keep their hair trimmed above their collars, their ears showing, clean shaven, and sideburns well trimmed.

Girls will let their hair grow long without trimming or thinning.

God's Word also teaches us how we ought to dress.

His Word tells us that any immodest clothing such as mini-skirts are out (I Timothy 2:9).

His Word says that it is important to Him that men dress like men and women dress like women (Deuteronomy 22:5).

His Word in the same verse tells us that for girls to wear slacks or other male-copied articles, or for fellows to wear frilly, feminine-type clothing is an "abomination" (a hateful and detestable thing) unto the Lord. This also goes for uni-sex style clothing, alike for both fellows and girls.

Why should God feel so strongly about the way we dress?

God made men to be real men, women to be real women, and no crossing over! God does not want soft, sissified fellows, or bold, mannish girls. God's plan is that girls should be feminine and modest, boys strong and protective.

"But I don't want to be an odd-ball," you may be tempted to say. "The way all the other fellows and girls dress and wear their hair is not the way the Bible says. If I dress and wear my hair like the Bible teaches, all the kids will call me a square."

Let me ask, Are you ashamed of Jesus? Would you rather please the ungodly or please Him?

God is concerned about our identification—about whether our dress identifies us with His church or with the sinners. God does not want us identifying with the ungodly. Any Christian who dresses to appear like a sinful group identifies with them, and God said that "if any man love the world, the love of the Father is not in him" (I John 2:15).

If a man doesn't want the sheep to think him a wolf, he shouldn't walk among the flock on hands and knees with a wolfskin on!

There is a Christian custom (I Corinthians 11:16), and God's people should dress according to that custom. The question we should ask is, Does my dress say "I belong to this world?" Or does it say "I am separate from the world, I belong to God?" Your dress identifies you with the group you most like, the godly, or the ungodly.

May our hearts be so in love with Jesus that we will desire to please Him in our dress, in the way we wear our hair, and in every other way too.

....

Women Cutting Their Hair

QUESTION:

Isn't there a verse in the Bible that says a scissors isn't supposed to touch your hair even to trim it one-half inch?

ANSWER:

Probably the verse to which you refer is I Corinthians 11:15: "But if a woman have long hair, it is a glory to her: for her hair is given her for a covering." In the Greek the word for "long hair" is *komao,* which literally means "to let the hair grow" (Thayer, Bullinger). The underlying thought is for the hair to be absolutely uncut, for if the hair is trimmed we are not letting it grow as the God of nature allows it to grow. God has given to the woman her uncut hair as a covering.

Let us notice verse 6: "If the woman be not covered," that is, if she does not have the covering of uncut hair because it is trimmed, then "Let her also be shorn; but if it be a shame for a woman to be shorn or shaven, let her be covered." What the Lord is saying is that a woman might just as well shave all the hair off her head as to trim it. God counts a woman trimming her hair to be sin as if she cut it all off and shaved her head.

I am sure you realize that it would be wrong for you to shave your head and then try to worship God. That is just the way God feels about your trimming your hair. Even one-half inch!

•••••••••••

"Broided" Hair on Women

QUESTION:

In I Timothy 2:8-10 does "broided hair" mean that if we Pentecostal ladies use "brush wool" or hair pieces in fixing our hair that we are doing wrong?

ANSWER:

The word *broided* (or *broidered*, Greek *plegma*) is an obsolete word meaning "embroidered." The applicable meaning of embroidery according to *Funk and Wagnalls New Practical Standard Dictionary* is "any variegated or elaborate decoration or ornamentation," and the verb *embroider* means "to embellish, to adorn, to exaggerate." The *Comprehensive Desk Dictionary* adds this meaning: "to add imaginary details to."

It is therefore plain to see that it means more than merely a simple and plain plaiting or braiding of the hair.

179

It actually refers to more than the hair itself, but to the manner of making up the hair, including the head-dress. Dake adds in his notes on *plegma,* ancient head-dress: "The hair was worn in the back in braids—from one to a record of 110 braids. In each braid would be woven silk cords with gold coins at irregular distances and reaching down to the knees, glittering at every movement of the wearer. Sometimes hair was made into temples, and other fanciful figures with the aid of gum. Sometimes caps completely covered with coins or frontlets ornamented with diamonds were worn."

Other translations of I Timothy 2:9 help us here:

> *"The adornment of a Christian woman is not a matter of an elaborate coiffure" (Phillips).*
> *"And not with wreaths or gold ornaments for the hair" (Twentieth Century New Testament).*
> *"Not with plaitings and ornamentations of gold" (Emphasized New Testament).*
> *"Not with (elaborate) hair arrangement or gold" (Amplified Bible).*
> *"Not with elaborate hair-styles, not decked out with gold" (New English Bible).*

Of course, the Bible teaches that our women should have long, uncut hair, and that the men's hair should be short (I Corinthians 11:4-15). I am happy that we as a movement adhere to these principles. I think the question stated above stems from the fact that in the past some ladies, particularly younger ones, wore their long, uncut hair in huge, exaggerated piles on top of their heads. Some of these elaborate hair-dos were artificially built up into mountainous masses and were an excessively elaborate fruit of pride and contrary to holiness. These certainly come under the heading of "broided (embroidered) hair," and are condemned.

This practice became so widespread and common in some places that many ladies felt that they had to keep up with the style and therefore added "brush wool" and hair pieces when they thought that their hair was too thin to put up properly.

My conviction is that a neatly combed, simply fixed hair-do without all the added "fixin's" is more pleasing to the Lord than an artificially built-up hair-do. By this I do not mean to suggest for ladies to be like the "hippie" girls who let their hair string down, oftentimes half blinding them, filthy, uncombed, and dragging in their food when they eat. Certainly no godly woman would want to look so disreputable. But I am equally convinced that hair-styling should not be excessively fancy either. And our women should not be made to feel that the thing to do is to keep up with a certain "Pentecostal" high-style, and resort to artificial aids in order to do so.

. . . .

Jesus Was Not a Nazarite

QUESTION:

Why is there so much objection to long hair for men and boys today, when Jesus was a Nazarite who therefore had long, uncut hair? The pictures of Jesus show that His hair was long.

ANSWER:

The desire of men and boys to have long hair is evidence, not that they desire to be like Jesus, but that they want to be like the world.

Your premise that Jesus had long hair is faulty on three points.

1. Jesus was not a Nazarite. He was a Nazarene, a very different thing. A Nazarene was a person from the city of Nazareth, while a Nazarite was a person such as Samson who was under a special vow, which consisted of abstaining from three things: (1) partaking of the fruit of the vine, (2) touching a dead body, and (3) cutting hair. (See Numbers 6:1-6.)

Jesus, not being a Nazarite, drank of the fruit of the vine (Luke 7:34), touched dead bodies (Luke 7:14), and therefore, not being under the law of the Nazarite He did not observe the third prohibition of not cutting the hair. The fact that cutting the hair was prohibited to the Nazarite is evident proof that for men to cut their hair was the accepted custom of the Jewish nation.

2. The pictures of Jesus do not accurately portray the physical likeness of Jesus or the customs of His day. They are totally imaginary, and undoubtedly false. God did not intend for us to have an accurate picture of how Jesus looked in the days of His flesh, for He knew that if we did men would make a god of His likeness and bow before that instead of worshiping Him in the Spirit. Yet man is determined to worship a physical form, so pictures, statues, and crucifixes are made and used in religious rituals and forms. But all these are purely the product of man's imagination. God's plan is shown in I Peter 1:8: "Whom having not seen, ye love. . . ."

Further, these pictures showing Jesus with long, flowing, feminine-looking locks of hair are contrary to the customs of the day. The likenesses of those contemporary with Jesus as shown in the statuary of the ruling power of Palestine, which was Roman, shows that the custom of that day was for men to have short hair, much shorter than in the popular pictures of Jesus. Only women wore long hair such as the pictures show Jesus wearing.

3. Jesus would never go contrary to His own Word. God's Word says, "Doth not even nature itself teach you, that, if a man have long hair, it is a shame unto him?" (I Corinthians 11:14). Nature, the Word of God, and both Jewish and Greco-Roman custom all agree together: Jesus did not wear His hair long! No matter what the customs of this perverse day are, God's Word stands forever.

••••••••••••

Preachers and Sideburns

QUESTION:

I knew a young preacher who came before the district board for a local license and he had long sideburns. He was rightly told by the board that he had to cut his sideburns before he could get his license.

Most Pentecostal pastors teach that it is wrong to wear long sideburns or hair that is over the ears or long in back. They said that to wear these things is to follow the trends of the world, and the Bible tells us to be a separate people.

As a young man I feel this is the right stand to take. But I have found it rather hard to convince other young men that long hair is wrong when they can see preachers with long hair.

Long sideburns, long hair, and a mustache is usually worn with pride. The Bible says pride goeth before destruction and a haughty spirit before a fall. Do you feel that there is too much pride creeping into our churches and into the ministry, and that this is one of the ways the devil is trying to stop the work of God? Do you feel that the ministers need to be examples to the young men coming up who will be leading the churches of tomorrow?

ANSWER:

I do indeed! It is grievous and tragic when ministers no longer conduct themselves in such a way as to inspire the saints to a higher, holier, nobler walk with God.

Even young ministers are counselled, "Be thou an example of the believers, in word, in conversation, in charity, in spirit, in faith, in purity" (I Timothy 4:12). How much more the older, more mature, and I trust, deeper in God should be "ensamples to the flock" (I Peter 5:3).

But while I say this I would add one word of warning to you. Look out for your own spirit that you do not get into a condemning or critical attitude toward the ministry, or that you presume to judge another man's motives. As a young man, you must respect the ministry and leave the dealing with them to those authorized to do so or to God.

You can get into such a condemnatory spirit that your usefulness for God will be seriously impaired. Never forget that when David, already anointed of God to be king in the place of Saul, so much as snipped a strip from the hem of Saul's garment his conscience smote him deeply, even though Saul had so grievously sinned that he had become a reprobate.

David realized that as long as God allowed Saul to be king he should honor him and leave him in God's hands. No wonder David was "a man after God's own heart."

·············

Dice and Cards

QUESTION:

Is it wrong to play games with dice and cards? I was taught against it, but it seems to be OK with so many now.

ANSWER:

I think that a good rule in playing games is to avoid the use of any paraphernalia that is commonly used for evil purposes such as gambling.

It should be obvious to anyone passing by that you are not engaged in playing games that are used by the devil's crowd for sinful purposes. It should never be necessary to make explanations.

Poker chips, roulette wheels, regular playing cards, and dice all fit into this category. Games that use these items should be questioned. They are mostly games of chance first and skill second. And they could be a stumblingblock to others, especially young Christians who have been delivered from the vice that uses these things.

Having said this, I hasten to add that all card games are not to be considered evil. If the cards are not the "playing cards" used for poker, bridge, etc., they could not be classified as cards popularly used for gambling. In fact, there are a number of wholesome Bible games that use their own cards. And there are also perfectly innocent family games which, although cards are used, the cards are distinctive cards made for that particular game.

In closing may I suggest that young people should be encouraged to play games where the element of skill is the predominant factor in winning, and not mere chance. Chess and checkers are illustrative of these games. The winner deserves to win because of his skill, and not merely because he is "lucky." Upgrade your games into this area, and you will avoid "the appearance of evil."

Home Movie Films

QUESTION:

Do you think it is all right for Christian people to check out from the public library western movie films or other old comedy movies or mysteries like Sherlock Holmes?

ANSWER:

I suppose I am a little old fashioned, but I fail to see the difference between viewing a movie twenty to thirty years old and one made last week. Twenty or thirty years ago the old film was new, and men who walked with God and had scriptural convictions stood tall and straight in pulpits and preached against them. Why should these same films be acceptable now?

The philosophy of relativism has invaded our thinking, I am afraid. "These films are old ones, and not as filthy and corrupt as the new ones, so I do not see any harm in them," is the rationalization involved. Comparing them with that which is more corrupt does not make them less impure than they were when they were first shown in the movie theaters of our land.

God's standards of separation, holiness, and purity remain the same. "Be ye holy, for I am holy," said the One who also declared, "I am the LORD, I change not." If viewing these films was wrong twenty or thirty years ago, it is wrong today! To holiness-minded Apostolics, relativism is wrong, and so is Sherlock Holmes!

●●●●●●●●●●●●

Movies in the Church

QUESTION:

I am a backslider, but I've been thinking a lot lately of returning to God. My problem is that I don't know what church I should attend.

I was planning to return to a church close to where I live. But today I found out some very disturbing news about that church—they now show movies for the young people at the church. And I mean real, full length worldly movies from Hollywood.

I was raised in Pentecost and was taught against movies and worldly television programs. So I'm wondering if I would ever become spiritual again attending a church that allows these activities, or if I could ever look up to the pastor as a spiritual leader.

Should I even try to return to this church? There is a Pentecostal church about thirty miles from us; should I go there?

I can't believe churches have become so worldly in the past two years, or have they? Please tell me what you think I should do. I'm very confused at this point, and I do need to "pray through" very soon and I need some spiritual guidance.

ANSWER:

I am glad that you desire to return to the Lord. Your life will never be complete out of the will of God. Repent, pray through, get a refilling of the Holy Ghost; and then by all means you must have a church home to attend faithfully and a pastor to help you in your spiritual life.

I can understand your dilemma in choosing a church. I am sorry some churches that used to stand strong and firm on lines of separation from the world have begun to compromise. Please let me assure you that the United Pentecostal Church does not condone or endorse in any way the showing of Hollywood films in any of our churches.

I would suggest that you investigate further before believing the report you heard. Many times tales are carried to destroy the influence of godly men and clean churches. Please be absolutely sure that what you heard is true and correct before you believe it.

If it should prove out to be true that this church is actually showing films of the type shown in theatres, then by all means do not associate yourself with this church. And if it should be that it is also connected in some way with the United Pentecostal Church, then I am indeed sorry and ashamed. It is certainly an indication that that church and pastor is in an awful Laodicean condition and that they will be spewed out of the Lord's mouth (Revelation 3:16).

I am happy to say that the great majority of churches that are affiliated with the United Pentecostal Church love old-fashioned Bible holiness and separation from the world. It is not the name "United Pentecostal Church" that will take you to heaven, but it is in obeying God's Word and living a holy life. I am sorry to say that it is undoubtedly true that there are some "foolish virgins" among us.

One pastor was accused by a denominational preacher of being bigoted and narrow-minded because he believed that only the Jesus Name people would make it to heaven. He replied, "I'm even narrower than that. I don't believe that all of us are going to make it." And I agree. As the song says, "The lukewarm and the backslider won't wear the marriage gown." However, I rejoice that as a movement the United Pentecostal Church stands for living a holy life unto God, hating the things of the world and abstaining from them, and doing those things which will prepare God's people for the soon return of our Lord Jesus Christ.

Associate yourself with, and faithfully attend, a clean, godly United Pentecostal Church that stands for a life of separation and holiness, even though you may have to travel a few extra miles to go there. It will pay eternal dividends!

In closing, may I urge you not to postpone the step of returning in full surrender to the Lord. Your soul is too precious. Do not let what others may do cause you to stumble. Stand by the truth! Go to the church where you know the truth is preached, *and practiced,* pray through, and then submit yourself to the godly pastor as he directs you in your spiritual welfare. "It will be worth it all when we see Jesus!"

....

New Converts and Television

QUESTION:

We are new in the Lord and can't seem to understand why we must obey our pastor and give up television.

ANSWER:

To you and all new converts I would say: Make a clean break with the world. When you draw close to God, television programs will appear cheap and shabby. You will begin to see through the eyes of holiness, and television shows will appear foolish and corrupt to you.

Television has been called a "vast wasteland." At its best it is a waste of precious time, and at its worst it is the champion of everything God hates. When you regard it as it really is, you will positively loathe it as a demon-inspired mortal enemy of your soul.

Obey your pastor. He knows what stand to take concerning owning a television set and all the other modern sins and practices. "Set your affection on things above, not on things on the earth" (Colossians 3:2).

Preaching on Television

QUESTION:

What is your opinion of using television to preach the gospel to the unsaved or to advertise the church, so long as we do not condone television for the saints?

ANSWER:

I have never regretted the positive stand against television which the United Pentecostal Church took in our General Conferences at Columbus and Tulsa. "It seemed good to the Holy Ghost and to us" then, and God has not changed His mind since!

God's approval has rested upon our organization as a result. Other groups who vacillated or merely mealy-mouthed on the issue have joined the toboggan slide of compromise and have become just like the denominations in their acceptance of carnality and worldliness of all kinds into their churches. Once the door is opened just a crack, there is no stopping the flood.

To illustrate, in 1905 some farmers in California decided to divert a small portion of the Colorado River into their irrigation canals for use on their farms. They knew it was a risk to tamper with the mighty surge of the river, but they were confident they could control and limit the amount of water they diverted.

However, the great river was too much for them. Their efforts to divert only a small stream resulted in the entire river turning from its natural bed and surging un-controlled across their farms and ranches, destroying and laying waste to the very lands they had hoped would be benefited.

For two years the great Colorado flowed out of control across hundreds of square miles of farmlands, cutting a new river bed, inundating homes, towns, and valuable stands of timber, and finally emptying into the Salton Sea, 200 feet below sea level.

Only by an act of Congress appropriating millions of dollars was the great river finally turned back into its original course. Whole freight trains, including locomotives and boxcars were dumped into the breach. These drastic measures finally brought the river under control.

But oh, the devastation left in the wake of this tragic experiment! The Salton Sea stands to this day as a monument to man's folly.

I predict that all who stoop to use television as a means of evangelism will sooner or later be swept away by the worldly tide which they think they can control, but which will eventually control and destroy them! They will inexorably succumb to the siren song of crowds, praise, money, and "mass evangelism." And the tragic thing is that they do it in the name of "Endtime Revival," under the guise of "soulwinning" and "reaching the lost." Perhaps they are sincere, but they are sincerely wrong, and their cloak of holiness and zeal may deceive others.

When a person uses television to reach people, he is putting his approval upon it. He cannot consistently oppose it. He is opening the floodtide, and the result could well be the unloosing of a great river of worldliness, carnality, and lukewarmness into his church, inundating the congregation with the awful tide of last day Laodicean apostasy.

Years ago one of our leading ministers was captivated by a child preacher and the large, curious crowds that came to this boy's meeting. He became so enamored of the glitter, showmanship, and appeal of reaching large numbers of people that he began to resort to questionable practices, even to deception and lying. When I remonstrated with him he replied, "My object is to get people to God; the methods are secondary and unimportant." We are hearing this kind of talk today.

I am fearful of this philosophy. It is the philosophy of the television user. Use any method, any means, just so you reach the people. The end justifies the means. This was the philosophy of the "Watergate Gang." But the Bible is against it.

God said that the method to be used when the ark of the covenant was to be moved was by staves upon the shoulders of the Levites (Numbers 4:1-15). But when David brought the ark back from the Philistines, he used the Philistine method of putting it on a new cart (II Samuel 6:1-3; I Samuel 6:7-8). The result was that God was displeased and struck a man dead even though he was sincere (II Samuel 6:6-7). When an ungodly expedient is used in the service of God, the inevitable end is tragedy.

David realized his wrong and said, "None ought to carry the ark of God but the Levites: for them hath the LORD chosen. . ." and, "because ye did it not at the first, the LORD our God made a breach upon us, for that we sought him not after the due order" (I Chronicles 15:2, 13).

With God the methods we use are all-important! Using television to preach the gospel is the Philistine's cart. It can result in nothing but disaster for God's people.

How foolish and futile it is to think we can temporize,

dally, and compromise with that which pertains to the enemy! Use Saul's armor to fight Goliath? David was too wise for that.

Let us take our stand, unashamed, for God's way, for holiness, and for truth. Genuine revival comes through old-fashioned prayer, fasting, and consecration accompanying the preaching of the gospel. Signs, wonders, and miracles are still in God's program. Crowds will gather as at Pentecost when the real thing is present. The pseudo-revival of the TV screen is sick compared to the glories of a real revival when it is actually taking place.

Away with the Philistine's cart of television! God's ark of "Endtime Revival" can never be brought in that way. Genuine revival will never be programmed on a TV screen! It will come using God's methods!

•••••••••••

Video in the Home

QUESTION:

Our pastor teaches against television and does not have one. But he and some others in our church have home video. At first this was for making videos of the family, church services and other similar uses. But later some of the church members began getting films at the library. Then they rented video films and made copies of them. It has now come to the point where a lot of these video films are the same ones that are shown on TV. What is the difference? Seems like one might as well stay up late watching the late show as to stay up late watching some of the

same things on video. Isn't this just a substitute for TV?
Your opinion please.

ANSWER:

I have been told that the United Pentecostal Church is the only church body of any consequence that has officially taken and maintained a definite stand against the television menace. We were alert to this insidious evil before it really spread over our nation, and God helped us to deal with it head on. I am thankful that the great majority of our fellowship continues to support that stand to this very hour. As a whole we are stronger and more united on this issue today than we have ever been.

One of the dangers we face today is complacency. Because one battle has been won we are apt to think the war is over. Not so! We may have successfully defended against one evil, but if a person really wants to find a way to do something he desires to do, but knows to be wrong, the devil will always help him find a way.

And so here comes a seemingly innocent toy—home video. "We can control video and use it only for edification and innocent pleasure, not like TV, all of whose channels are in the hands of the devil," is the reasoning.

As you have indicated in your letter, one step seems inevitably to lead to another. Before we are really aware of what is going on, the innocent toy can become a stumbling block and a tool to bring the same evil into our homes which we thought we had whipped in another guise.

While we guard the center of the line, Satan may be making an end run, and we find ourselves outflanked and defeated. Video has many attractive features, and can be used for good purposes, but when it is used as you describe we are certainly violating the spirit, if not the letter, of our position against television. And, yes, it does become a substitute for TV.

If video is ever to be acceptable to holiness-minded people, it can never be used without clear guidelines and restrictions. It seems to me that these have been made by the United Pentecostal Church at a recent General Conference. These guidelines call for video to be used strictly for family and church purposes and rejects any use other than these. It must not become a means to provide carnal and worldly entertainment.

In closing, may I say that we tend to grade on the curve. Because other groups and movements are so cold and so worldly we may think that our lukewarmness is acceptable to God because it is warmer than the freezing temperature of others. But God does not grade on the curve. His standards are forever fixed. It always has been, is today, and always will be a narrow way (Matthew 7:13-14), a way of "holiness, without which no man shall [ever] see the Lord" (Hebrews 12:14). We will never find a curve in *that* standard.

•••••••••••

Gossip in the Church

QUESTION:

The church I was in before I came into Pentecost was filled with gossip and ungodly talk. Everything seemed hypocritical, and I was disgusted. I knew there was a better Christian life for me. When I found Pentecost I was happy and thought that all the saints were holy, almost like angels. However, now I find that some people in the Pentecostal church gossip just like the members of the church I left, yet they testify, shout, and claim the victory. I am disillusioned and discouraged. How can people filled with the Holy Ghost act like the people of the world? Is Pentecost real after all?

ANSWER:

Your experience has been repeated many times in the lives of other new converts. I am sorry that it has to be that way, for it is all unnecessary. But in order for you to understand, let me make a few observations.

First, the new birth experience does not automatically make anyone perfect. What it does is to wipe out the past completely and to give one a new start. A new convert is thus as an infant entering into a new life. What that new life becomes, however, is largely up to him. But the Holy Ghost makes available to him all the resources of heaven, to help him make his new life a life of victory and blessing.

There are three things given the Christian to lead him on into perfection. These are the Holy Ghost, the Word of God, and the ministry.

Therefore we are told, *after* our Pentecostal experience, to "be filled with the Spirit" (Ephesians 5:18). We are told to be "doers of the word, and not hearers only, deceiving your own selves" (James 1:22). We are told to "obey them that have the rule over you, and submit yourselves: for they watch for your souls" (Hebrews 13:17), since they are given to us by God to perfect us (Ephesians 4:11-12).

If one does not allow these three things to operate fully in his life, he will revert back into being the kind of person he was before he was saved. If he was a gossiper before, he will be a gossiper again; if he was a liar before, he will be a liar again.

And so Christians are told that an overcoming life is not something that comes automatically, but that we must diligently do some things after receiving the Holy Ghost. There is a "putting off" and a "putting on" that must be done. Permit me to quote Ephesians 4:22-32 from *The Living Bible:*

> *"Then throw off your old evil nature—the old you that was a partner in your evil ways—rotten through and through, full of lust and sham. Now your attitudes and thoughts must all be constantly changing for the better. Yes, you must be a new and different person, holy and good. Clothe yourself with this new nature. Stop lying to each other; tell the truth, for we are parts of each other and when we lie to each other we are hurting ourselves. If you are angry, don't sin by nursing your grudge. Don't let the sun go down with you still angry—get over it quickly; for when you are angry you give a mighty foothold to the devil. If anyone is stealing he must stop it and begin using those hands of his for honest work so he can give to others in need. Don't use bad language. Say only what is good and helpful to those you are talking to, and what will give them a blessing. Don't cause the Holy Spirit sorrow by the way you live. . . .Stop being mean, bad-tempered and*

*angry. Quarreling, harsh words, and dislike of
others should have no place in your lives. Instead,
be kind to each other, tenderhearted, forgiving one
another, just as God has forgiven you because you
belong to Christ."*

The new birth is the starting point, and it is only as
one progresses in God that the carnal practices (such as
gossiping) are overcome. The Holy Ghost does not force
one to be good, to quit lying, backbiting, etc. But the Spirit
is given to us to empower us, to "help our infirmities"
or weaknesses (Romans 8:26). Therefore it is only as we
draw upon the power of the Spirit through prayer, fasting,
obedience, faithfulness, and faith that we are enabled to
overcome our weaknesses.

It is certainly not God's will for His church to be filled
with carnality and gossiping. Neither should you stumble over those weaker than you who indulge in this practice. Maintain a high spiritual level in your own life, take
your eyes off others and get them on Jesus, and you
may be used of God to lead them into a higher plane of
spiritual life and victory.

Yes, Pentecost is real, the most wonderful reality in
the world. But God does not force any individual to live
right. Each one must "work out [his] own salvation with
fear and trembling" (Philippians 2:12). The Holy Ghost
is not given because one is perfect, but to "guide [lead]
you into all truth" (John 16:13). If a person will let Him,
God will enable him to put off all carnal practices and
become more and more like Jesus.

We are to set the example and God will use us to lead
others into a blessed life of overcoming power where the

works of the flesh have no place whatsoever!

●●●●●●●●●●●●

Girl Staying at Boyfriend's Home

QUESTION:

What do you think of a girl filled with the Holy Ghost who goes to her boyfriend's house to visit him and stays there for a week? How about a boyfriend who spends his vacation at his girlfriend's home? The father and mother are apostolics, and so are the young people.

ANSWER:

Although I'll probably be called hopelessly outdated, I cannot help but cringe when I see Christians conform to the world and its loose standards and think nothing of it.

I realize that such conduct is apparently an acceptable thing these days. But at the risk of offending parents and young people, let me just say that as for me and my house and on behalf of truly holiness-minded people, such actions are unthinkable. To be thrown together in such close proximity for several days and nights has certainly the "appearance of evil" and could lead to tragedy and heartache. Parents need to lift a standard for their children in the fear of God.

If such a visit is deemed expedient, the one visiting should stay at another house or at a motel, never in the same house with the boyfriend or girlfriend.

Girls Accepting Gifts

QUESTION:

What gifts should a girl accept from her boyfriend? I know some girls whose boyfriends buy them clothes to wear, expensive gifts, and give them money. My mother thinks this is not right. What do you think?

ANSWER:

I am with your mother. Self-respecting girls still do not accept presents of clothing, expensive gifts, or money. Such presents should be returned with a polite note saying in essence, "Thanks, but no thanks."

....

Hanging Around the Gang

QUESTION:

Is it wrong for a person who has been delivered from gangs to go to places where there may be a few gang members the person used to know?

ANSWER:

For a person, even one who is filled with the Holy Ghost, to deliberately expose himself to the same environment and pressures which had overcome him before is foolish indeed. Your natural self is evidently attracted by the atmosphere of the gang. Peer pressure was probably a contributing factor to your becoming involved initially. God was good to you to deliver you and give you a new life.

It is sad but true that some people have been lured by their former companions back into the sinful life from which God had delivered them.

Peer pressure is powerful! The approval and acceptance by others is a tremendous force, oftentimes for evil. It has great drawing power, as powerful as the attraction of drink to an alcoholic.

Let me give you a sadly neglected verse of Scripture which warns against evil associations: "Do not be deceived and misled! Evil companionships, (communion, associations) corrupt and deprave good manners and morals and character" (I Corinthians 15:33 *Amplified*). This is an absolute divine law. You cannot escape it. If you run with bad company it will corrupt you.

It is the part of wisdom to avoid those who would not be good for you to associate with. Choose your companions carefully. Do not hang around that which is a temptation to you. The wise man aptly expressed it:

> *"Enter not into the path of the wicked, and go not in the way of evil men. Avoid it, pass not by it, turn from it, and pass away" (Proverbs 4:14, 15).*

May you be as wise!

4
Finances

Figuring Tithes

QUESTION:

I borrowed $400 to buy a truck and turned around the next day and sold it for $700. I paid back the $400 loan. Do I pay tithes on the $300 profit or on the full $700? Also, if I buy a home for $30,000 and rent it out for $300 a month, do I owe tithes on that $300 I make for rent? It is just enough to make my payments.

ANSWER:

I am glad that you feel obligated to pay tithes, and I do appreciate your sincerity in knowing how to compute the proper amount of tithes.

The key verse of Scripture that helps us to know on what basis tithes are to be computed is Deuteronomy 14:22. This verse tells us that tithes are to be computed upon the "increase" portion of our income; that is, in case of sales, upon the profits. The same principle holds in all other kinds of income. Costs incurred in the obtaining of the income are deducted from the gross, then tithes are paid on the net, or "increase."

Therefore, you should deduct your costs from the selling price of the truck, leaving the profits, or "increase" of $300 on which to pay your tithes.

In the case of the house, the purchase price of the house is not to be taken into account, for you are not selling the house. Your payments on the house are just like putting money into a savings account at the bank. When you sell the house you will receive the money back.

The rent you receive should be tithed with the

understanding, however, that all of your costs incurred in the operation (not the purchase) of your house be deducted first. These would include taxes, insurance, upkeep, etc. The remainder is increase, and must be tithed.

It is important to realize that all the increase of your income, whether wages, profits, or dividends should be tithed, and it is out of this increase on which you have already tithed that the payments on your house are to be made.

It is tremendously important that you be very diligent in your tithing, and that in figuring the increase any items you deduct from your gross are actual expenses you incur in the making of the money, such as the purchase price of the item you sell, and not deductions for some other cause.

When these scriptural guidelines are understood, tithing becomes a very fair and equitable (as well as biblical) method of fulfilling your basic financial requirement toward the Lord. However, tithing is but a start. God's plan is tithes *and* offerings (Malachi 3:8). Let us not try to short-change God! He has given His all—how can we do less than be faithful in our tithes and offerings to Him?

....

"I Cannot Afford to Tithe"

QUESTION:

The money I receive is just the amount of my rent,

utility bills, and living expense. How can I pay tithes? I have tried to pay tithes but I get behind on my bills. There is simply no way I can afford to tithe on the very little that I get. I have been told if I don't pay tithes I will be lost. I am troubled. Please advise.

ANSWER:

These are days of financial trial for many people. Not long ago I visited a very poor home of a poverty-stricken couple. Neither of them had worked in over a year, and they lived from hand-to-mouth on welfare. They had just the previous Sunday asked for financial help, and said they did not have enough funds for groceries to last the week out.

To my amazement, when I entered their house, I saw a very large and expensive television set. I asked if they were having problems making the payments, and they assured me that the TV was one thing they would make sure they paid for even if they had to go hungry to do so. They were astonished that I would even suggest they forego the television in order to be able to have money for food, and became quite abusive when I left the house without giving them money.

Now, I am sure that you do not, like this couple, rob God of His tithes in order to use it in some ungodly way. In fact, I am reasonably sure you have told me the truth, that you genuinely feel that you cannot afford to tithe. Nevertheless, you do need help to see things as you ought to, and that actually you are not letting the Lord help you with your finances. In other words, in robbing God of His tithes you are robbing yourself!

Let me bring to you a few pertinent points for your

consideration, and then see if we cannot find an answer to your dilemma.

First of all, none of us have an option as to whether or not to pay tithes. God's Word is very plain. The tithe is not ours, it is God's. To withhold the tithe is committing an act of robbery, stealing someone else's money, and that someone else is God Himself (Malachi 3:8). I am sure you would not resort to holding up a service station or a bank at gunpoint to obtain money to pay your bills. Yet you are unashamed to say (in essence) that you have robbed God! Then you ask, as though there were the possibility that I could somehow get God to absolve you of paying Him what is His, "How can I pay tithes?" There is simply no alternative; the tithe money in your purse is not yours and you have no business keeping it or using it in any way—it belongs to God.

Second, God loves you and wants to supply all your needs. He does not supply your needs in accordance with the amount of money you get in your monthly check, but He supplies "all your need, according to his riches in glory by Christ Jesus" (Philippians 4:19). When the Lord is your Shepherd you can say with David, "I shall not want" (Psalm 23:1).

You may ask why this has not happened to you. Has God failed to keep His Word with you? Never! Even though you have robbed God and added that loot to the amount that He has allowed you to have, the total of those two amounts is still not enough to provide your needs. And may I add, it never will be. This brings us to the third point.

All of God's promises are conditional. In the letter to the Philippians, Paul praised them for their generous giving (Philippians 4:14-18). They had given out of their deep poverty (II Corinthians 8:1-2), beyond their ability (verse 3), pleading with Paul to accept their giving (verse 4). As a result of their liberality they were probably destitute and possibly in debt. It was to these people that the Holy Ghost through Paul made the marvelous promise that God would supply, not a reward of $10.00, $100.00, or $1000.00 for their generosity, but that God would supply *all their need,* no matter how great it might be, and no matter how little they had.

We are likewise told in Matthew 6 not to worry about food or clothes or other needs that we all have because God would supply them (verses 25-32). But please notice that this promise again is conditional: "But seek ye first the kingdom of God, and his righteousness; and all these things shall be added unto you" (verse 33). Only as we honor God first will He work on our behalf to add to us all our needs.

If you want God to supply your needs, He must come first. "Honour the LORD with thy substance, and with the firstfruits of all thine increase: So shall thy barns be filled with plenty, and thy presses shall burst out with new wine" (Proverbs 3:9-10). Instead of saying you can't afford to tithe, you should be saying that you cannot afford *not* to tithe.

The principle of tithing is not that God needs the money. "The earth is the LORD'S and the fulness thereof" (Psalm 24:1). One purpose for which God ordained tithing is so that He may become a partner with the tither in order to bless him and supply all his needs. To the tither He said, "Prove me now herewith, saith the LORD of hosts, if I will not open you the windows of heaven, and pour you out a blessing, that there shall not be room enough to receive it. And I will rebuke the devourer for your sakes, and he shall not destroy the fruits of your ground; neither shall your vine cast her fruit before the time in the field, saith the LORD of hosts" (Malachi 3:10, 11).

You see, tithing is for the benefit of the tither. God binds Himself by His promise—He is duty bound to supply the needs of the one faithful in tithes and offerings. God will see to it that the nine-tenths of the money you have left will go farther with God's blessings upon it than all of it without His blessing. In fact, God will miraculously stretch it out to meet your needs. You cannot afford not to tithe.

In closing, let me point out to you that these promises are for those who give cheerfully, not grudgingly (II Corinthians 9:6-7); and for those who give in faith (Hebrews 11:6). Then, although you may still live from hand-to-mouth, it will be from God's hand to our mouth!

••••••••••••

Offerings Beyond the Local Church

QUESTION:

If one pays tithes faithfully to his church, is it OK to give offerings where you feel it is most needed?

ANSWER:

In addition to tithe you have an obligation to the

church expense fund and to missions and outreach programs. If, after you have faithfully tithed and given these offerings to your church, you wish to give offerings to other worthy causes connected to God's work, by all means do so.

•••••••••••

Tithing on a Small Income

QUESTION:

What would you advise people on a small fixed income to do about tithing? I am on welfare, and I have a child to raise. I recently had a terrible accident and lost all I had. It will be very hard for me to give any large part of my limited income to the church.

ANSWER:

Some time ago I clipped this excerpt from an unknown source which expresses in beautiful words an answer to this question: "Too many persons miss an exciting adventure with God because they assume they must meet their needs entirely from their own resources. Jesus offers a bold alternative, almost too good to believe.

"He invites us to get to know Him and His righteousness, and to build up His kingdom. Then He promises to *make Himself accountable* to meet our needs! Now, that's a bargain! Our needs will be met, not from our poverty, but from God's infinite resources. You can read about this astonishing offer in Matthew 6:25-34.

"We demonstrate that we are willing to step out into this adventure of faith when we return to the Lord a tenth of His gifts to us. It is our part of the partnership. It is our way of acknowledging that all our income came from Him in the first place, and that we trust Him to make the remaining nine-tenths meet our needs.

"Our heavenly Friend understands poverty. During His journey here on earth He had no place to lay His head (Matthew 8:20).

"When we look at our pocketbooks, we might all say, 'How can I afford to give?' When we look at the privilege of partnership with God, we can all say, 'How can I afford *not* to give?' The difference is the direction we are looking."

May I add that tithing is not giving to the Lord of your means. It is simply returning to the Lord that which is not yours at all, but His, and which He has declared is holy unto Himself (Leviticus 27:30). Not to tithe is to be a robber, and most of all, a robber of God (Malachi 3:7-8).

Yet, lest we tithe only out of fear, God has promised rich blessings on those who tithe (Malachi 3:10-11). "The devourer" is Satan, and when God says He rebukes him for my sake, it means that He delivers me from Satan's power! And then He challenges us to prove Him! You will find yourself ahead spiritually, physically, mentally, and financially when you tithe. Prove it out! You will find that instead of not being able to afford to tithe, you cannot afford *not* to tithe!

• • • • • • • • • • •

Tithing on Social Security

QUESTION:

I heard that if one was working when they begin paying tithes on their earnings, that after retirement and you are on Social Security (I'm not talking about S.S.I.), your monies are free from tithes, as they were paid while you were working. Is that true or not? Also, does one pay tithes on an inheritance?

ANSWER:

A good rule to follow, which applies in this case as well as other cases, is the one enunciated in Deuteronomy 14:22. Here the Lord told the Israelites who tilled the ground: "Thou shalt truly tithe all the increase of thy seed, that the field bringeth forth year by year."

The key phrase is "all the increase." This means that tithes should be paid on everything that comes to you that is an increase over that which you previously had. It does not say that it must be wages or commissions or profits from sales. It says "increase," which includes any and all of those things as well as from any other source which adds to or increases that which you previously possessed, whether it be wages, gifts, inheritance, commissions, profits, or whatever.

Of course, if you are retired and are now receiving monies on which you have previously tithed, you do not have to pay tithes again on those particular amounts. These could be considered the same as money you have previously received, paid tithes on, and banked in a savings account. If you withdrew these funds, you would have to pay tithes only on the interest you received since you had already tithed on the amounts you had banked.

However, that which you are receiving after retirement which you did not pay tithes on, such as the amounts contributed by your employer, must still be tithed by you as you receive them.

In the event you did not pay tithes on the amounts taken out of your paycheck and which you are receiving now, you need to tithe on these amounts also.

I suggest you be exceedingly careful that you keep accurate records and that you are careful that the tithe of "all your increase" is paid. When the books are opened and men are "judged out of those things which are written in the books" (Revelation 20:12), can you say for sure that one of them will not be a ledger?

•••••••••••

Stewardship of
Large Amounts of Finance

QUESTION:

I will shortly be coming into a considerable sum of money from the sale of my business which I sold because I do not want my time to be so completely taken up with business affairs. It is my desire to use what time I have left for the glory of God. My problem is that upon receiving this large amount from the sale of my assets it will be subject to taxes to the extent it almost amounts to confiscation; that is, a large percent will be going to the government. I could reinvest in tax-sheltered investments, but do not wish my time taken up taking care of investments. Do you have any suggestions? Does the Bible give any guidance in a matter like this?

ANSWER:

Yes, indeed, the Bible does give guidance in matters of this kind. God's Word gives us principles that are changeless, and as relevant today as when they were written hundreds of years ago because they came from the heart of a loving God for the express purpose of guiding us in making decisions such as the one facing you today.

Jesus addressed Himself to matters involving finance more than to any other subject because He knew the terrific snare of the love of money. One of the outstanding teachings Jesus gave concerning the wise use of money is found in Luke 16. The passage that many people simply ignore because they do not understand it is found in verses 9-12. And yet these verses give us some of the most profound and important teachings in all Scripture concerning the wise use of money. Because much of the richness of the meaning of this passage is lost in translation, here is a paraphrase that will help make the meaning clear:

> *"My counsel to you is, use your worldly wealth that is so often used in wrong ways, to change enemies of God into your friends (that is, to win souls to Christ, for they will then become your friends for all eternity). Then when money is no longer valuable, your friends (who have already gone to heaven) will welcome you there.*
> *"He that is faithful to use little sums wisely*

215

> *and well can be depended upon to use things of*
> *great value wisely and well also, but he that is*
> *careless and who cheats in small matters cannot*
> *be trusted to handle a large amount of money.*
>
> *"So if you have proven careless or untrustwor-*
> *thy in your use of the money God has allowed you*
> *to have, how can He ever trust you with that which*
> *is of true and eternal value?*
>
> *"And if you have proven untrustworthy in*
> *your use of that which was only lent to you (by*
> *God), how can He allow you to have possessions*
> *of such great value that they will last eternally?"*

You see, it is very important that we use the money God allows us to have wisely and well for the glory of God. As He puts wealth into your hands He also places a great responsibility upon you. If through your neglect you allow the government to take a large percent of the money when it is in your power to turn it instead into channels that would win souls into the kingdom of God, I am afraid you would come into condemnation and suffer great spiritual loss.

Let us look at some scriptural guidelines to follow as a true child of God.

I am sure you know that first of all tithes must be paid; that is, ten percent of all profits or "increase" (Deuteronomy 14:22) should be paid as soon as you receive it. The pastor must take this money (which may still be a very large amount) and be as careful in the use of it as you must be in the ten times larger amount you have to account for. God has placed it into his hands, and he has a God-given responsibilty to see that he uses it wisely. (See Numbers 18:21, 26-28.) This is your first step, and it must be taken whatever you decide to do with the remainder.

The question now is, What are you going to do with the ninety percent remaining so that you will please God and obey what He has told you in Luke 16? By all means, it is important here that you counsel with your pastor. But may I make some observations and suggestions.

One of the reasons God has blessed our nation so greatly in spite of its failures and terrible slide down into the morass of corruption and immorality is that it gives consideration to those who give to God's church. Up to fifty percent of your adjusted gross income may be given to the church or to a recognized charity, and it is an allowable deduction on your income tax. In no other nation of the world can you do this.

Your next concern should be your local church. In prayer and counselling with your pastor, determine how much to give. After you give, always take your hands off. It is no longer yours, and it is now the responsibility of others to see that it is used properly.

Next, there should be gifts to the many wonderful soul-saving programs of the United Pentecostal Church, such as Foreign Missions and Home Missions. Great advances can be made by our missionaries if we assist them with our giving. At the same time, you will be a wise steward. Your wealth will be used to win souls into the kingdom of God. Their salvation will make heaven rejoice, and you will meet them as your friends there, for they would not be there if you had not given to send the gospel to them.

These generous gifts will undoubtedly enable you to

drop into a lower tax bracket and pay much less in taxes to the government.

You will probably be tempted at times not to give very much. Satan will tell you not to tithe or give large amounts. Your auditor and your attorney may not know the Lord as you do and therefore may not think it wise for you to give so much to the church, but you know what God's Word says, and you know what God wants you to do, so do it! It will be a source of great joy to you. Tell these men what you want to do, and have them work out a program of giving that will please God, will gain you true riches, and will save you from paying such a large sum to the government.

Of course, you do have responsibility to your family for their needs to be met (I Timothy 5:8). When you honor the Lord with your giving He will give you wisdom as to how you should invest the remainder in such a way that your needs and those of your family will be met. Again, get some professional help in making the proper investments for your purpose.

I believe that by taking heed to these scriptural guidelines your money will be paying dividends of true value that will never cease through all eternity!

•••••••••••

Stewardship of Small Amounts of Finance

QUESTION:

I read with interest your reply to the fellow who had

*more money than he knew what to do with. That's not my
problem. I'd sure give to the Lord if I had it but I don't.
I'm really strapped all the time. My question is, How do
you keep from getting bitter when others have so much and
you have so little?*

ANSWER:

This age-old problem is still with us. It is not always
easy to understand all the whys and wherefores. Many
have puzzled over it, and frankly, I cannot say I have all
the answers. Nevertheless, the Word of God does give
us enlightenment in this difficult area.

Three thousand years ago David struggled to find the
answer. In Psalm 73 he confessed that his feet "well nigh
slipped" when he "saw the prosperity of the wicked"
(Psalm 73:2-3). In succeeding verses he expressed his
bewilderment as he beheld how God permitted others to
prosper while he was "plagued all day long and chastened
every morning" (verse 14); and he concluded, "When I
thought to know [understand] this, it was too painful for
me" (verse 16).

Then the answer came! But it only came when he
"went into the sanctuary of God" (verse 17). "Then", he
said, "I understood their end." You see, there are some
things that we can never perceive until we look at them
through spiritual eyes and weigh them out in the light
of eternal values.

In eternity things will assume their proper perspective. The rich man becomes poor and the beggar rich. (See
Luke 16:25.) Things really make no sense until God
straightens them out in His eternity. Only if there is a
hell and a heaven can there be rhyme and reason to the

inconsistencies of life.

But there is another answer to this riddle, an answer that will not have to wait for eternity for us to understand. It is so easy for us, shortsighted as we are, to envy those in more favored or affluent circumstances than we.

Perhaps you remember the old tale about Damocles, who longed to enjoy the bounties he saw to be the lot of Dionysius the Elder. Whereupon Dionysius invited Damocles to take his place on his throne and be regaled with all the pleasures and honors accorded a king. In the midst of the entertainment, however, Damocles happened to look upward and perceived a naked sword suspended over his head by a single hair. The awareness of the fact that accompanying the lavish pleasures of the throne was constant peril symbolized by the impending sword filled him with terror. Damocles was delighted to return the throne to Dionysius, and slip back into the comparative security of his former low estate.

Did not Paul write Timothy, "They that will be rich fall into. . .a snare, and into many foolish and hurtful lusts, which drown men in destruction and perdition" (I Timothy 6:9).

If we only knew things as God does, we would know that it is best for us to accept with thankfulness the condition and situation He permits us to be in. It is far better for us to "be content with such things as ye have, for he [God] hath said, I will never leave thee nor forsake thee" (Hebrews 13:5).

Paul discovered the beautiful secret of contentment in God. He possessed the joy of knowing that he was in God's hands; and he accepted as from God whatever lot in life he found himself in. His faith in God with respect to material possessions is expressed in Philippians 4:11-13:

> *"Not that I speak in respect of want: for I have learned, in whatsoever state I am, therewith to be content. I know both how to be abased, and I know how to abound: everywhere and in all things I am instructed both to be full and to be hungry, both to abound and to suffer need. I can do all things through Christ which strengtheneth me."*

What wonderful victory! What blessed peace of mind! Instead of rebelling against his lot, he thanks God for it, knowing that he is in God's hands, and that whatever is best for him God will provide.

I hope you will find this place of faith and assurance in God. Seek the Lord for His grace to help you. What you have in God is worth more than all the gold and silver in the world. "Godliness with contentment is great gain" (I Timothy 6:6).

In closing, may I call your attention to a portion of your letter that really concerns me. It may be that it reveals some of the reasons why God cannot trust you with more wealth. You say, "I'd sure give to the Lord if I had it, but I don't." I'm reminded of the little poem,

> *"It's not what you'd do with a million*
> *If riches should e'er be your lot,*
> *But what are you doing at present*
> *With the dollar and a quarter you got?"*

Jesus said, "He that is faithful in that which is least is faithful also in much: and he that is unjust in the least is unjust also in much" (Luke 16:10). If God cannot depend upon you to thank Him and be content with what He permits you to have instead of complaining, and if He cannot depend upon you to be faithful in tithes and offerings with the little you have now, why should He ever entrust you with more? If you will not honor Him with what you have, the chances are very slim that God will ever let you have any more.

If you do not repent and begin serving the Lord with the material things He presently permits you to have, you will probably continue to be in the same destitute circumstances for the rest of your life, all the while wondering why others should be more favored both financially and spiritually than you. But the reason is within your own spirit. Think about it.

5

Marriage
and
Family Life

Is a Marriage Ceremony Necessary?

QUESTION:

My fiance and I feel that God has made us for each other. Of what necessity is a marriage ceremony and a preacher pronouncing us man and wife since it is God who has joined us together as Mark 10:9 states?

ANSWER:

The evolutionary hypothesis that we are merely animals that have evolved from a lower to a higher order has colored the thinking of this generation. We are told that marriage has lost its usefulness, that we can mate indiscriminately, and as the animals we are, we need not be beholden to the authority of a Higher Power. Give full reign to all of our instincts, we are told.

While the questioner apparently does not subscribe to that philosophy, nevertheless the thinking behind the question has been influenced by this degraded concept. The proof is easily seen if you substitute the evolutionist's "nature" for the word "God" in the question.

Mark 10:9 does not even hint at the elimination of a wedding ceremony. The context plainly shows the very opposite. The question was asked Jesus (verse 2), "Is it lawful for a man to put away his wife?" It is evident that these people were lawfully married, and therefore the word *wife* is used. Verse 4 informs us that to break this marriage there had to be a writing of divorcement under Moses' law. There would be no necessity for this legal document unless there was an official bond to the marriage which it would take a writing of divorcement to break. To have this bond necessitates a wedding and a ceremony with vows exchanged which bind each to the other. Only thus could the lady be called "wife" as in verses 2 and 7.

Verse 7 says a man is to "cleave to his wife." Only then are they called "one flesh" (verse 8), and joined together by God (verse 9). Remember, this is spoken of a man and his lawfully married wife, not of two people "shacking up" without a wedding ceremony. God does not join such together.

In Bible days "the selection of the bride was followed by the betrothal which was a formal proceeding. . .confirmed by oaths. . . . Between the betrothal and the marriage a varying interval elapsed. During this period the bride-elect. . .was virtually regarded as the wife of her future husband. . . .At the marriage ceremony the bride moved from her father's house to that of the bridegroom" *(Peloubet)*. Today we eliminate the period of time between the oath-taking and the marriage, and make the exchange of vows a part of the wedding ceremony. However, in both cases it is a formal ceremony with the exchange of sacred vows in a legally recognized procedure.

Man cannot eliminate marriage without paying a fearful penalty. Every attempt to displace marriage with some other arrangement has ended in disaster. Marriage did not originate in the minds of men for the sake of convenience. God is its author.

It is certainly noteworthy that Jesus began His public ministry at a marriage in Cana. He sanctified and endorsed marriage by His presence, and there He performed His first miracle.

Civilized people everywhere recognize that marriage

is of sacred origin and therefore to be entered into with appropriate solemnity and the exchange of vows before a qualified officiant. The one performing the marriage actually represents God who authored marriage and performed the first ceremony in the Garden of Eden. Therefore, although marriage may be just as binding legally when officiated by a justice of the peace or some other person in an authorized secular position, yet children of God who want to honor God in their marriage go to God's house and have the minister perform the ceremony in a sacred atmosphere.

Then, certainly, the blessing of Mark 10:9 can be yours.

•••••••••••

Whom God Has Joined Together

QUESTION:

Is it not love that makes a marriage and not a piece of paper (license)? Does God join a man and woman together just because a man says, "I now pronounce you man and wife?" The Bible says whom God has joined together let not man put asunder.

ANSWER:

Of course, every marriage should be a love match, and husband and wife should love each other with a pure, strong, unselfish love. God's Word says that the older women should teach the young women "to love their husbands" (Titus 2:4). Men are to love their wives "as

227

Christ loved the church" (Ephesians 5:25), and "as their own bodies" (Ephesians 5:28).

Yet most marriages in Bible days did not begin as love matches. Very often the parents arranged the marriage, and oftentimes the bride and groom were actually strangers until their betrothal and marriage.

Such was the case of Isaac and Rebekah. Isaac's father Abraham sent his servant to find a bride for Isaac. He brought Rebekah back to Isaac who had never seen her before. Genesis 24:67 tells us that he then "took Rebekah and she became his wife, and he loved her." He married her *before* he loved her, but he *did* love her!

While we do not advocate such arrangements, it is equally true that God would never command a man to love his wife unless it were possible for him to do so. Remember, God told husbands to love their wives "as Christ loved the church." Jesus loved us when we were completely unlovable, sinners and enemies of God (Romans 5:8-10). Most wives are not that difficult to love! Any man can love the wife he has, else God would not have commanded it.

The Bible does not teach that there must be love before there is a valid marriage or one that God recognizes. The Bible teaches that a man is to love the wife he has, and you may be sure that God will help you do what He commands you to do. "His commands are His enablings!"

When Jesus said, "What God hath joined together, let not man put asunder" (Mark 10:9), He was referring to the institution of marriage, to the joining together of a man and his wife into one flesh (see verse 8). It is hoped that love is present, and it will be if a man obeys God's

Word. But whether love is present or not, when a man and woman are joined together in the institution of marriage (which God is the author of), and they become one flesh, the Word tells us that God has joined them together by this means, and they must never permit man to put them asunder.

The false teaching that a marriage was not made in heaven if a man and his wife do not love each other and therefore they can separate and find new mates is a hellish doctrine and contrary to every principle of holiness and sound doctrine. It has spawned tragedy, heartaches, broken homes, adultery, and "free love." There is no more unscriptural teaching polluting God's church today than this. I believe most of the false teachers who advocate such things are men with reprobate minds who "creep into houses, and lead captive silly women laden with sins, led away with divers lusts" (II Timothy 3:6).

In closing, if you are married and love is not as strong as it should be in your marriage, instead of thinking that maybe the answer is to leave your companion and find another one to love, settle it that your marriage must never be put asunder. If you will draw near to God, He will help you to really love your companion.

Do not wait for your mate to love you. If you will initiate the love as Christ did when "He first loved us" (I John 4:19), you will find that love will be reciprocated, and your marriage can truly be a happy one when you bring Christ's love into it.

••••••••••••

Guidance From Ann Landers

QUESTION:

I read Ann Landers in our daily paper. Lately she has been dealing with sex. My daughter is seventeen and I have told her to read it also because I believe she has some good answers. My pastor says it is wrong, that I should be the one to teach my daughters about such things. In fact, he warned us not to read her column. I believe he is narrow-minded. He says it is garbage. Am I right?

ANSWER:

No, you are wrong, tragically wrong on at least three counts: (1.) in your responsibility to your daughter; (2.) in your estimation of Ann Landers, and worst of all, (3.) in your judgment of the man in whose hands God has placed the responsibility for your soul. Let us take these points one at a time.

1. *Your responsibility to your daughter.* For you to turn over to an unsaved person the teaching of your daughter in matters of right and wrong in such critical matters as sexual morals and behavior is not wise for one who claims to be a Christian. This is a responsibility God has placed in your hands. Guidance in matters of sex should be given by parents in a godly atmosphere and with spiritual emphasis.

Ungodly people think mostly in terms of the physical aspects of sex, and are conditioned by such ungodly philosophies as "situation ethics." It is your responsibility before God to instruct your children according to the Word of God in a godly, wholesome manner.

2. *Your estimation of Ann Landers.* She is a brilliant, witty, and articulate woman with a remarkable ability to turn a phrase. But the answers she gives are not guided by the Holy Ghost. The highest level of her moral and spiritual aptitude is too low for a child of God.

One without the Holy Ghost is not qualified to guide God's people in matters such as sexual morality. God made our sexual natures, and we need to be guided in these matters by those who know Him.

The old delusion of the devil in the Garden of Eden is repeated endlessly that somehow we are missing out unless we partake of "the knowledge of good and evil" (Genesis 3:5). Ann Landers, Dear Abby, and others like them are modern trees of good and evil, mixed. Some good at times may come forth, but it is always tainted with carnal reasoning and it is never wholly clean. It is like taking a piece of pie out of the garbage can.

It seems to me that you have become warped and spoiled in your thinking. God's Word warns us: "Beware lest any man spoil you through philosophy and vain deceit, after the tradition of men, after the rudiments of the world, and not after Christ. For in him dwelleth all the fulness of the Godhead bodily. And ye are complete in him. . ." (Colossians 2:8-10). Notice this: *complete in Him!*

Do you really believe you are complete in Christ and what He and His church offers, or do you also need such advisors as Ann Landers?

3. *Your judgment of your pastor.* You reject the advice of the man in whose hands God has placed the watch-care of your soul and that of your daughter's. Your rebellious attitude prevents you from seeing things as God sees them, and as your pastor sees them. And so you call

your pastor "narrow-minded." I hope he will continue to be "narrow-minded" to teach that only the narrow way leads to heaven!

May I remind you in closing that God's Word says to "obey them that have the rule over you, and submit yourselves: for they watch for your souls. . ." (Hebrews 13:17).

You had better obey your pastor in this matter, for of one thing I am sure: Ann Landers is not ordained of God to watch for your soul!

••••••••••••

Teenage Intimacy

QUESTION:

My teenage daughter has been raised in a Christian home and school. She is going with a teenage boy and they both claim to be Christians. I found out recently that they have been intimate. I have talked with her, and restricted her, and I'm fasting and praying for her. What else can I do? I can't bear the thought of her being lost!

ANSWER:

Undoubtedly you are a conscientious Christian parent that deeply loves your children. It is heartbreaking when children break over the traces and do things that bring sorrow and tragedy into their own lives and the lives of those who love them. These are days that try men's souls.

Needless to say, your daughter cannot be a Christian and still be involved in fornication. She is lost unless she truly repents, which not only means being sorry, but being sorry enough to quit her sin, and look to Jesus for forgiveness and cleansing.

I feel for you as a parent. Do not abdicate your responsibility toward your daughter. Love her, get close to her, try to establish genuine communication with her, but also be firm with her. Try to lead her to repentance until she abhors the thought of a repetition of her sin.

Tragically too many teenagers are swept away by peer pressure, and will not listen to their parents. The spirit of the age is, "Do your own thing. You do not need someone else to tell you what is right or wrong or to tell you what or what not to do."

Many of our churches try to establish rules and guidelines for the teenagers to adhere to in their relationships. And if the church does not have these rules, the parents should. One important rule is that which involves chaperones and curfews. If young people were properly chaperoned at all times, and curfews established, they would have little opportunity for illicit behavior. This is doubly important now since she has already crossed over the line, and it would give her support in not repeating the sin.

It is not only necessary that both these young people repent and receive a refilling of the Holy Ghost, but they need to understand that they cannot be allowed to be alone together again. They should not resent this ruling.

By all means tell your pastor. He is given to you for times like this. Through his walk with God, knowledge of the Word, and experience, he will know how to talk to these young people and help them. He will also help you as a parent to know what to do to help your daughter so that she will want to be the kind of person she ought to be.

Even though the kind of conduct she has been engaged in can destroy her whole future and her chances for a happy, normal, married life, it need not do so if she truly repents, puts this behind her, and lives a godly life from here on. Let your pastor and his wife help her. And ask God to give you help and wisdom during these trying days. Mix faith in with your fasting and prayer. Sometimes parents must travail in birth twice for their children! (See Galatians 4:19.)

•••••••••••

Afraid to Marry

QUESTION:

I am a young minister engaged to a fine Spirit-filled girl. We had prayed through about our marriage, and God had given us both assurance it was His will. The date was set, but suddenly she grew fearful and cancelled our wedding plans. She says she still loves me, but is fearful of making a mistake. She will not talk about it. I still love her and feel it is God's will for us to marry. I am at a loss to know what to do. What do you suggest?

ANSWER:

This problem is similar to one asked me some years ago by a young Christian who felt she was backslidden.

I asked her what sin she had committed. She answered that she had not committed any sin that she knew of, but just felt tormented and condemned. I then asked her what particular thing she was condemned over. She did not know, but just felt a general feeling of guilt and condemnation, and she was sure God had abandoned her and she was lost.

Now, this is one of Satan's devices (II Corinthians 2:11). I explained to her that if it was God dealing with her and condemning her, the Holy Ghost would put His finger on the sin she had committed and she would know what it was that she had done wrong so that she could repent of it. God does not torment us or toy with us like a cat with a mouse. His infinite love reaches out to us to help us. If we have sinned He will let us know exactly what the wrong is without a shadow of doubt.

But if Satan cannot get you to sin, his trick is to make you think you have. He tries to put a spirit of condemnation on a believer, and tries to make him believe he has sinned. If you accept it, you live in fear and doubt, your faith is gone, and you cannot believe God. But the condemnation Satan puts on you is different from God's, and this is how you will know it: Satan's condemnation does not pin-point the wrong—it is just a vague feeling you cannot identify. Do not accept condemnation as from the Lord unless you know what it is for, for that is the only way God works!

If you feel condemned but cannot ascertain for what after searching your heart and praying, resist the devil in Jesus' name, because that condemnation is not from God—it is from the devil!

The same principle holds true in the problem you have

with the young lady to whom you are engaged.

If you both sincerely love each other, and you are both filled with the Holy Ghost living for God and there is no scriptural impediment to your marriage, and you both have prayed through about it and know it is the will of God for you to marry, then any fears that one of you may have is from the devil to tear you up and disrupt the will of God for your lives.

However, if there is a basis for these fears, that is another matter. She should not withhold the reasons from you. She should tell you exactly what the problem is so that it can be worked out together. It is wrong for her not to talk to you about it. If her fears are a warning from God, they would have a tangible basis; you would both be mistaken in receiving God's assurance that it was His will, and the reason would be sound enough for not proceeding with the marriage.

But a tormenting fear which is not based upon anything but a feeling, after you have already received assurance from God and there is no scriptural impediment, is a satanic trick to disrupt the will of God for your lives. If she gives in to it, she will become a prey to fears and torments from the devil in other matters later in her life.

The key is to know the will of God, and then not let nameless fears and terrors turn you aside from fulfilling God's will for your life. As I stated, if the fear is from God, the Holy Ghost will reveal the reason for it unmistakably, and you will be led by God, not by a pointless tormenting feeling which is Satan's method.

One last word of warning. Be sure you know it is the will of God, not just your own human desire. Then move ahead confidently. God does not contradict Himself. But be gentle, be kind with her. It is natural for her to be fearful of making a mistake. After all, it is the most important step of one's life after salvation. Take your time. Go slow. Do not force her. Help her in love. After all, you will have a long life together if the Lord tarries. Your patience and understanding mean much now. Our prayers and concern are with you both.

•••••••••••

Perversion in Marriage

QUESTION:

Is it possible for a husband and wife to commit perversion?

ANSWER:

I Corinthians 7:4-5 lays down the principle that the wife's body belongs to her husband, and the husband's body belongs to his wife; and Hebrews 13:4 declares that the marriage bed is undefiled. There is another verse of Scripture equally inspired of God which should regulate our conduct within the bonds of marriage. In I Thessalonians 4 we are told that we ought to know how to walk in such a way as to please God (verse 1). The verses which follow explain the walk that pleases God.

Verse 3 tells us first of all to abstain from fornication. The Greek word is *porneia* from which our word *pornography* is derived. It means unlawful sexual conduct, harlotry, or whoredom, whether the individual is married or unmarried.

Verse 4 adds that we should know how to possess our bodies (vessels) in holiness and purity. According to I Corinthians 7:4, this would also include one's mate's body also.

Verse 5 warns us that in "possessing our vessels" we are not to do so as the Gentiles (unsanctified and unholy heathen or sinners) do, for they do so "in the lust of concupiscence," or unbridled sexual excesses of a depraved or abnormal nature. Every Spirit-filled person should realize that his body and that of his companion's, are temples of the Holy Ghost, and they are to be used as God intended and not for some perverted or unnatural lustful desire.

Caresses are normal and natural within marriage, and are certainly nowhere condemned in Scripture. But whatever the caresses, they should lead to the normal marriage relationship and never take its place through perverted desire.

•••••••••••

"God Will Forgive Me For Leaving Her"

QUESTION:

Before we were married my husband agreed for us to have children. Now when I mention wanting children he says he won't love the child and that he'll leave me. He says that God is a loving and merciful God, that He'll forgive him for leaving me. Is that a Christian, Spirit-filled attitude?

238

ANSWER:

No, it is not. Frankly, it appears that your husband is an immature, self-centered boy wearing man's clothes. His childish concept of God, if it were not so tragic, is laughable. It is presumption to think that one can willfully, deliberately sin, and then expect God to forgive just because we want Him to.

Forgiveness only follows a genuine sorrow and regret for sin, and a turning from it in abhorrence, coupled with a desire to rectify the damage that has been done. Planning to sin, presuming that God will later forgive, negates the first principle of repentance, which is that you must hate the sin and turn from it.

Paul, in his second epistle to the Corinthians, commended them for their genuine repentance. First of all, they "sorrowed to repentance" with a godly sorrow (II Corinthians 7:9-10). You cannot repent unless you are genuinely sorry from the heart, and without repentance there is no forgiveness.

Then Paul described the effects of their repentance. The depth of it was so great that it wrought in them "carefulness. . .a clearing of [them]selves. . .indignation [at their own sin]. . .fear. . .vehement desire [for God and His holiness]. . .zeal. . .revenge [making things right]" (verse 11). These are the fruits of a genuine repentance that God accepts, and He therefore extends forgiveness to that individual.

I sincerely hope that your husband will change his attitude and accept his responsibilities like a man, and most especially, like a Christian.

Divorce and Remarriage

QUESTION:

Could you give me Scripture on divorce and remarriage? How can a born-again Christian leave a companion he has loved (apparently) and lived with for years, be separated one month, and go to Tijuana and marry a new acquaintance? Do not Christians fast and pray for God's divine will in marriage anymore? Why do saints of God delight in gossip and in seeing someone else's marriage falling apart?

ANSWER:

It always grieves me, and I am sure it grieves God, when I hear of people in the church having marital problems which they cannot seem to reconcile. It is doubly tragic when this leads to a break-up of the marriage, divorce, and a remarriage. This is not God's will for His people.

Jesus said in Matthew 19:9: "I say unto you, Whosoever shall put away his wife, except it be for fornication, and shall marry another, committeth adultery: and whoso marrieth her which is put away doth commit adultery."

The only grounds God will recognize for the breakup of a marriage is fornication *(porneia)* or unfaithfulness by one of the partners. Then and only then is divorce permissable in God's eyes, and remarriage on the part of the innocent party.

You ask several questions, most of which I cannot answer, not knowing all the circumstances. It appears that you have been deeply hurt. But you must find your help in God. Do not lash out at the other saints of your church—you need them more now than ever. It is the devil's business to make us think that everyone is against us. But I am sure most of them are praying for you and not gossiping as you may think.

I am also sure that your pastor stands ready to help you through this difficult time. Go to him and let him counsel you. Give yourself to prayer, and rededicate yourself to God.

In closing, let me remind you of the time a lion attacked Samson in the vineyards of Timnath (Judges 14:5-6). By the help of the Lord he slew that lion. Later as he was returning that way he turned aside to view the lion's carcass. To his surprise, he discovered that a swarm of bees had built their hive in that carcass. He reached in, filled his hands with the honey, and went down the road eating it.

The tragic experience you have undergone may seem to be destroying your life just as the lion attempted to destroy Samson's. But God gave Samson all the strength and grace he needed to overcome the lion, and He will give it to you in this hour of your need. The battle may not be easy; it may be long and bitter, but if you trust the Lord He will help you win the victory over discouragement, bitterness, and despair. You can kill that lion, through Christ!

It may not be right away, but there will come a time in your life if you stay true to God, that you will be able to reach down into this tragic experience and extract handfuls of honey. God can do this for you if you put your hand in His and let Him lead you through this trial and then on out into a deeper and more wonderful place in God than you have ever had before. God bless you!

•••••••••••

"How Can I Get My Husband Back?"

QUESTION:

I am married and have two girls. My husband and I broke up because he found me with another guy. Why I did that I do not know because I really love my husband. I have been going to church and really praying. All I want to know is how can I get my husband back? Please help me.

ANSWER:

You say you are going to church and praying, but your letter does not say whether you have fully repented or not, or whether you have received the Holy Ghost (either the filling or the refilling) since you sinned. Praying is a good start, but that is not enough unless it is followed up by obedience to the Word and a consistent Christian life.

You allowed the devil to move into your life. For a married woman to be seeing a man who is not her husband is sin. You have sinned against God, against your husband, and against yourself.

Have you asked God to forgive you, and have you so deeply and sincerely repented that it will never happen again? God knows whether you are really sincere or not. If you genuinely and sincerely repent, God will forgive you. And if you seek Him with all your heart and soul He will fill (or refill) you with His Spirit. Then you can trust Him to help you concerning your husband.

Your letter also does not say if your husband is a Christian or not. However, I would suggest you confide in your pastor, tell him the entire story. If he sees you are sincere, genuinely sorry for the mistake you made, and have truly prayed through to a solid experience in God, perhaps he would feel that he could talk with your husband about a reconciliation. Oftentimes this approach has worked where nothing else will.

May God help you to be the kind of wife and mother you should be. Whether or not your husband returns to you, be determined to serve the Lord.

Fornication and Divorce

QUESTION:

Recently my husband backslid and departed from me. He claims he wants a divorce and then he says he doesn't. My greatest desire is to abide in the will of God through it all. I've counselled with my pastor and he believes I have every right to divorce him. He also believes I must be absolutely sure of the final decision. He has told me until I am certain of what the Scriptures declare I should wait on the Lord. I have his permission to write to you.

Concerning divorce, our Lord teaches us that "whosoever shall put away. . .except it be for fornication. . ." (Matthew 19:9). Paul wrote, "But if the unbelieving depart let him depart. A brother or sister is not under bondage in such cases" (I Corinthians 7:15). What is your conviction of these passages of Scripture?

My husband and I have been separated for five weeks. Am I to assume he has committed fornication when he won't admit it? Is depart an all-inclusive term for fornication? When a brother or sister is no longer under bondage, does that free me to get a divorce?

ANSWER:

I can certainly feel for you at this time of severe trial in your life. I know God's grace is sufficient, and that He will see you through.

I appreciate your fine pastor and his concern. He is a true man of God. I also appreciate your need to be sure what the Scriptures teach before you make your move. That is the part of wisdom. I do not have all the answers, I am sure. But perhaps I can point you to some divine principles found in God's Word which may help you.

I stand solidly upon Matthew 5:32 and 19:9, that fornication is the only ground upon which God accepts divorce. The purpose of scriptural divorce is simply to legitimize what God has already stated, that when one of the parties is guilty of fornication, the marriage vow is broken as surely as though he were dead. If the innocent party desires he or she may divorce and remarry, but only in the Lord.

Fornication is the translation of the Greek word *porneia,* from which our word *pornography* is derived. It literally means unlawful sexual indulgence, which in the case of married people we would term adultery. It also carries with it the thought of a continued and unrepentant course of action.

In I Corinthians 7:15 there is no divorce and no grounds for it, simply the unsaved mate departing to live outside the home. Unless the one who leaves commits adultery or divorces his wife (or husband) and marries another, the parties are still married, and the Christian partner is not scripturally eligible to get a divorce and remarry.

The "bondage" spoken of is not the bondage of marriage, but the bondage of condemnation for the breakup of the relationship. In other words, God will not hold you accountable for the actions of the other party, and you should not feel guilt for the fact that the home is not complete and your children are left without the guidance and discipline of a father.

You should not assume that your husband has committed fornication simply because he has left you. To depart is not the same as fornication. He is still your husband. You are a married woman in the sight of both God and man, and you should conduct yourself as a married woman.

Your first responsibility is to pray for your husband that he will be saved. If he gets saved, he will probably wish to return to you, and he may desire to return anyway. He is a very unhappy man, and perhaps God can reach him now.

If he stays away, he will probably eventually wind up either with another woman or apply for a divorce. He may want you to get the divorce, but I would refuse unless he acknowledges and confesses that he has committed adultery and wants freedom to continue. If he has another woman, you are then scripturally free to divorce him and remarry in the Lord; or if he divorces you and remarries, you are likewise free to remarry.

But the first move is his. Wait on the Lord. Generally you regret what you do in haste. It will come to a head sooner or later. Then you will know what course of action to take scripturally.

....

Unfaithful Husband

QUESTION:

My husband is a backslider. He left our home eight months ago and has been living with a woman ever since. He has filed for divorce.

I love my husband and there will never be anyone else in my life. Is he lost to me if he should get a divorce? I want to believe that God will bring us back together and refill my husband with the Holy Ghost. How do you know if it is God's will for him to go or to bring him back? If I have faith, will God do it? Or is it His will for me to walk alone?

Please help me understand how I can reach a place of full surrender to God.

ANSWER:

I certainly feel for you and understand your deep sorrow. A broken home is a sad situation for you. I am sure you love the Lord deeply and want His will more than anything else. It is commendable that you would be willing to forgive your husband and take him back if he would leave the other woman and return to you.

The question is not whether or not God could do as you ask. Of course He could. He is the Savior of sinners; He is the healer of broken homes and broken hearts. To ask whether it is God's will to save your husband or not, we need to go no further than II Peter 3:9 where we are assured that God "is longsuffering to us-ward, not willing that any should perish, but that all should come to repentance." It is not God's will for anyone to be lost, and that includes your husband.

Further, it is God's will for you and your husband to be together. He has plainly declared, "Wherefore they [husband and wife] are no more twain, but one flesh. What therefore God hath joined together, let not man put asunder" (Matthew 19:6). It is the two becoming one flesh, the marriage relationship, which is the bond by which God joins husband and wife together. Once the marriage is consummated, it is not the will of God that it should ever be sundered.

Yet, in spite of the fact that it is the will of God for all men to be saved, many are still lost. In spite of the fact that it is the will of God that husbands and wives should remain together, married people separate and homes are broken.

Man is the only one of God's creatures to whom God has given the power of moral choice. And God does not remove that power from man no matter what he does. If a man desires to sin, God will not stop him; and if a man wants to leave his wife, God will not compel him to stay, even though he is going contrary to God's will. God simply does not force anyone against his own will.

Therefore God will not force your husband to return to you. Hundreds of precious, godly women are continuing to live for God in our churches, even though their husbands have deserted them. They have found that the grace of God is sufficient, and they lean on the Lord for their strength, comfort, and companionship.

This does not mean you should not pray for your husband and trust God to save him. It is still true as the old song says, "He will not compel you to go 'gainst your will; He just makes us willing to go." As in the story of Jonah, God will send judgments upon the backsliders to bring them back. But in the final analysis, the choice must still be made by the individual involved.

By all means pray for your husband. Then leave all things in the hands of the Lord. Live for God one day at a time. There is still the chance your husband will turn and be saved. Events will determine what actions you should take. Whatever happens, the grace of God is sufficient for you.

May the Lord bless you and help you in the days ahead. Keep your hand in His. Stay close to your pastor and his wife. They will help you make the right decisions.

....

Can the "Guilty" Party Be Saved?

QUESTION:

Can the so-called "guilty" party who remarries ever be saved, if he has entered into an adulterous relationship, without repenting, separating from his second spouse and never marrying again? In addition, how about the sin-

nor who marries such a person? Does the marriage con-
stitute a continuous adulterous relationship, although both
parties may repent of their sins?

ANSWER:

I am sure you are aware that there are differing views
on the subject in question, even in the Pentecostal
fellowship. I do not presume to answer for others; nevertheless, I do feel the Scriptures answer your question, and
therefore I will endeavor to point out to you what I
sincerely believe is the scriptural answer, which is also
in harmony with the manual of the United Pentecostal
Church.

First of all, let it be plainly understood that adultery
is not the "unpardonable sin." It is a horrible sin,
loathsome to the utmost degree in the eyes of God, and
God has set it apart from all other sins. (See I Corinthians
6:18.) Nevertheless, it can be forgiven, and it was when
it was repented of in Bible days (I Corinthians 5; II Corinthians 2:1-11; 7:8-12). Any and every sin can be
forgiven if the guilty person will truly repent. Only if an
individual does not repent is the sin "unpardonable." Of
course, there could come a time in one's life, if he continually resists the convicting power of the Holy Ghost,
that he becomes incapable of repenting. At that point he
has committed the "unpardonable sin." (See Matthew
12:31-33; Ephesians 4:19; Romans 1:28; I John 1:9;
II Timothy 2:25; II Peter 3:9.)

Secondly, when an individual leaves his innocent
spouse and marries the second time, it is plain that he
is guilty of the sin of adultery (Matthew 19:9). The word
fornication used here is translated from the Greek word

porneia, the term of whoredom whether committed by married or unmarried people. In this verse it refers to a married person committing whoredom. Marriage is so sacred that it is not to be trifled with. The sin of "porneia," whoredom, causes the sacredness of the marriage to be broken. When one party leaves the marriage and marries again, he has committed fornication. It is important for us to understand that once this sin has been committed the former marriage has been broken completely and, even though the second marriage may likewise be broken, the man cannot return to his first wife (Deuteronomy 24:3-4). God says that is an "abomination" to Him.

Third, even though he may be the guilty party in breaking the first marriage when he married the second time, and in doing so committed the act of adultery, to remain in this marriage is not "living in adultery." He is not now bound to his first or former wife; that relationship is broken completely and forever. God forbids that he should ever go back and marry her again. Therefore his present wife is truly his wife and they are not now living in sin. They committed sin in marrying, but it cannot be undone. They are now "one flesh" and should remain married.

Fourth, there is no such thing as a "continuous adulterous relationship" if the parties are legally married. If there was a former marriage, it has been completely broken, and the second marriage is now binding. Jesus called all five men the adulterous woman at the well of Samaria had married her "husbands" (John 4:18). Even though she had sinned when she left the previous husband to marry another, yet that act effectively broke the former marriage, and the man she married became her lawful husband. Jesus said so! But when she took the sixth man, she may not have divorced the fifth, and it is certain that she did not marry the sixth, so he was not her husband. It is important that we understand this.

Finally, in the Old Testament the one guilty of committing adultery would be stoned (Leviticus 20:10; Deuteronomy 22:22). Then his or her spouse would be free to remarry, for the former mate was dead. Under grace we do not kill the offender, yet the same principle prevails. Because of his whoredom *(porneia),* the one divorcing and marrying another becomes dead to his or her first spouse. The second marriage now becomes binding and should never be broken.

Sin always is disastrous. It is a fearful sin to break a marriage. The first marriage should be the only marriage; it should remain inviolate, and both parties should remain true to their marriage vows. Reproach always follows a break-up of a marriage. There are terrible consequences. Let us save ourselves from this generation that Jesus called a "wicked and adulterous generation."

•••••••••••

Children's Prayer Life

QUESTION:
Should you expect children who receive the Holy Ghost with the evidence of tongues to have the same prayer life

*as an adult? Do they experience the same Holy Ghost? I
have a twelve-year-old granddaughter who received the
Holy Ghost, but she doesn't seem to have the same fervent
prayer and worship as most adults after receiving this
wonderful gift. Our pastor feels that because of the evidence
she has the Holy Ghost. I would like your answer.*

ANSWER:

The initial evidence of receiving the baptism of the
Holy Ghost is speaking in tongues as the Spirit gives utterance. It is spoken of as accompanying the baptism of
the Spirit in every account of someone receiving the Holy
Ghost where any sign is mentioned (Acts 2:4; 10:44-48;
19:1-7), and was indisputable proof to the apostles (Acts
10:45-46).

We are told in Acts 2:17-18 that in receiving the Holy
Ghost there is no distinction of race ("all flesh"), no
distinction of sex ("sons and daughters"), no distinction
of age ("young men" and "old men"), no distinction of
social classes ("servants" and "handmaids" were included). It is for the Jewish race and for the Gentiles, both
for those of the first century and for those of the twen-
tieth century, "even as many as the Lord our God shall
call" (Acts 2:39).

It is the same Holy Ghost that fills each one in
whatever station in life he may be. When one speaks in
tongues as the Spirit gives utterance, it is an evident token
he has received the gift of the Holy Ghost.

We must understand that while God makes no distinctions in race when He pours out the Holy Ghost, still the
black people remain black and the whites remain white.
Although God makes no distinctions in sex, still a male

remains male, and a female remains female. The young are still young in years, and the old are still old. The Holy Ghost does not change these things.

So a child receiving the Holy Ghost is still a child and immature. He is not suddenly transformed into a grownup, mature adult. He still likes to play, he is not ready to drive a car, he still needs to be taught discipline; in fact, he is the same boy he was before he received the Holy Ghost in his human development and characteristics. He still needs to learn obedience, self-discipline, and how to keep the victory. He still has temptations peculiar to boys his age. Paul wrote Timothy, "Flee youthful lusts" (II Timothy 2:22). Timothy had the Holy Ghost, but he also had desires and temptations which appealed to his youthful age and personality.

God does not instantly put an old head on young shoulders. He tells us to "grow in grace" (II Peter 3:18). Children and young people who are saved need to learn how to make themselves pray when they do not feel like it. Children naturally love to play, not to pray. The Holy Ghost never forces anyone to do something against his will. The power of choice is still in our hands.

It was said of the child Jesus that He "increased in wisdom [intellectually] and stature [physically], and in favor with God [spiritually] and man [socially]" (Luke 2:52). I believe that in His humanity He was as human as we are, and even the spiritual aspect of His life had to develop just as we should also. Do not expect your granddaughter to show maturity beyond her years. She needs your love, understanding and encouragement, not criticism.

It is vital that she learn the beautiful secrets of prayer

and worship. But don't compare her with adults. As a matter of fact, I know some "adult" Christians who do not have fervent prayer and worship either, and who are probably as immature as your twelve-year-old grandchild. They need to be helped, just as your granddaughter does.

Encourage her, pray for her, and set a godly example for her. And then, as the child Jesus, she will learn how to "increase. . .in favor with God" as well as man!

6

Public
Worship

Sunday Morning Job

QUESTION:

I am a Christian and attend church services through the week and on Sunday night. On Sunday morning I have a job. I was told this was a bad testimony and letting the Lord down. I thought we didn't keep a certain day, so why does it matter if I miss Sunday morning?

ANSWER:

When God's people gather together for service, every Christian should be present. We are soldiers in an army (II Timothy 2:3-4). We are in a state of war "against principalities, against powers [of the devil], against the rulers of the darkness of this world, against spiritual wickedness in high places" (Ephesians 6:12). Every service is a battle in that war.

What kind of a soldier refuses to go into battle? He is a deserter, a traitor to his country. In the army he could be subject to court martial and until recently, if he were found guilty, shot.

We are commanded to warn people not to forsake assembling together, because there would be so much the more of this sin as the day of the coming of the Lord approaches (Hebrews 10:25). This command is as much the Word of God as Acts 2:38!

We give our time and effort to that which we consider to be the most important. If it is not absolutely necessary for you to work on Sunday morning, to do so is an indication of your lack of love for Jesus and His cause. "He that loveth father or mother more than me

257

is not worthy of me," Jesus said (Matthew 10:37).

Someone has well stated, "That which keeps you from attending church will keep you from the Rapture!"

•••••••••••

Children Asleep in Church

QUESTION:

Could one reason many young people are withdrawn from living for God in our Christian homes be because they are allowed to sleep in church at an age when they need to hear the Word and get involved in the services?

ANSWER:

I realize that children need more sleep than adults. However, if parents would take the time and effort to insist their children take naps on the days when there are services, it would pay dividends in the spiritual lives of their children. Children can and should worship God right along with the adults, even though they might not understand everything that is said. If they were encouraged to be involved in spiritual matters, they would develop rapidly in spiritual understanding and interests and become tied to the church and learn how to live successful Christian lives at an early age.

One of Pharaoh's attempts at compromise with Moses was, "Go now ye that are men." In other words, Satan would have us think that only adults should worship the Lord. Moses reply was, "We will go with our young and with our old, with our sons and with our daughters. . .for we must hold a feast unto the LORD" (Exodus 10:9).

May we be as wise, and bring our children to the feast of the LORD!

•••••••••••

Bored in Church

QUESTION:

During service I find myself looking for things to occupy my time. People tell me it's my age (I'm sixteen years old). I don't know if it is a phase I'm going through. I just can't seem to pay attention to the services, I get bored. I don't want to be bored, it scares me. What should I do?

ANSWER:

You are right to be concerned. Certainly it is not normal for a New Testament Christian to be bored in church, at sixteen or at any other age.

If you are baptized in Jesus' name, filled with the Holy Ghost, have a healthy prayer life, and are active in soulwinning and outreach endeavors, you should never be bored. Really, church should be the most exciting activity of your life.

To be brutally frank and truthful with you, I do not think you are as interested in the things of God as you would like to think you are. Richter said, "A scholar knows no boredom." This is because a scholar is wrapped up in his studies. They are the most important thing in life to him. If the things of God are that vital to you, you would not be bored in church. Every service would be a new and thrilling experience to you. It is only because you are not really interested in spiritual matters that you are bored in church.

I hope you realize that your condition is not just a "phase" you are going through and that you will some-day automatically outgrow it. Please realize that it is a disease, and that it will become more virulent and dead-ly with the passing of time. It is terminal unless cured, and the Scripture calls it "carnality."

Let me see if I can describe your condition. You love to be entertained—you never get bored with that. But ser-mons turn you off; you want something "light, bright, brief, and brotherly." Sermonettes for Christianettes, don't-you-know. Plays, programs, and singing don't bore you, do they? But when the preacher gets up to deliver the Word of God, boredom sets in.

Jesus used another term to describe your condition. He called it being lukewarm, and declared, "I would thou wert cold or hot" (Revelation 3:15). To those lukewarm, He said, "I will spue thee out of my mouth" (verse 16).

Lukewarm people just can't seem to get excited or stirred up. They cannot rejoice in the Lord, neither can they weep over the lost. They are apathetic, bored. They are, as Leonard Ravenhill says in his book, *Why Revival Tarries,* lobotomized. He says:

> *For years this horrible operation (lobotomization) has been a weapon in the hands of dictators. Hitler used it on millions of his own flesh and blood. Stalin is said to have turned over ten million of his slaves into living Zombies with this simple operation, which takes only five minutes*

to porform. Afterwards the victim is said to be irrevocably insane.

The patient is strapped to an operating table, the straps tight and very strong. Electrodes are attached to the temples, three jolts of electricity are shot through the patient's brain, enough to start violent convulsions which finally give way to anesthetic coma. The doctor then takes his leucotomes (ice-pick-like instruments) and inserts them under the patient's eyelids. With a hammer he drives through the eye sockets into the fore part of the brain, severing the pre-frontal lobes of the brain from the rest of it. The result?—A Zombie (for want of a better word).

Fifteen Zombies can be made by science in ninety minutes. To add to this, we have the alarming news that there are probably 100,000 lobotomized people in the United States. . . .

Lobotomized people are incapable of emotion, conviction, or will. They just don't care. And some saints have allowed the devil to put his spiritual ice-picks under their eyelids. Really, this is what separates the foolish virgins who will be left behind when Jesus comes from the wise virgins who are ready for the coming of the Lord.

God has always been concerned that His people be fired up, red-hot for God. We should never sink into apathy or boredom. God picked up Ezekiel by the hair of the head and carried him from the River Chebar in the land of captivity back to Jerusalem and showed him the abominations being carried out there by the elders of Israel. Then in Ezekiel's sight God called for six men with weapons of slaughter in their hands to go forth and slay everybody in Jerusalem who did not sigh and cry for all the abominations which were being committed. Every apathetic, bored, unconcerned person was to be slain. That is what God thinks of those who allow this disease of luke-warmness and carnality to possess them.

What has happened to you is that you have left the fervent, burning love for God and His cause which you once had (Revelation 2:4). The *Amplified Version* puts it a little more plainly: "You have abandoned the love that you had at first—you have deserted Me, your first love."

You may ask what you should do.

I can do no better than to give you the advice of Jesus to the Ephesus church which had left their first love: "Remember therefore from whence thou art fallen, and repent, and do the first works [act as you did at first]; or else I will come unto thee quickly, and will remove thy candlestick out of his place, except thou repent" (Revelation 2:5).

I guarantee that if you do this you will not get bored or fall asleep in church again! Every service, every sermon, if you are in love with Jesus, should be and will be exciting to you, even greater and more thrilling than a visit with the sweetheart one is betrothed to marry!

• • • • • • • • • • •

Forgetting God on Vacation

QUESTION:

Recently I heard a young man (supposed to be filled with the Holy Ghost) telling a neighbor, "When I was on vacation I just forgot about church and did everything I wanted." This really stirred my heart. Are we teaching our young people that they can just come in and out as they please?

ANSWER:

This young man has a heart problem. Jesus said, "Thou shalt love the Lord thy God with all thy heart, and with all thy soul, and with all thy mind, and with all thy strength. . ." (Mark 12:30). You can never forget that which you love with all your heart. It is a measure of how little this man loves God if he can put spiritual things out of his thoughts. An individual who is walking in the love of God could never think of taking a vacation from the Lord.

I hope somehow that we not only teach our young people, but help them find an experience in God of such depth that it can only be described by that one wonderful word, *Love.*

• • • • • • • • • • • •

Should Sick People Come to Church?

QUESTION:

In all honesty, what is your opinion of sick people going to church? We know Jesus is our healer, but is it really wise to attend service with a high temperature and hacking bronchial cough that is extremely contagious?

ANSWER:

An individual may say he has faith for his healing, and come to church in the condition you describe, but for sure he cannot have faith for everyone else! Why should he infect all the people who do not have all the faith that he professes? It is the part of wisdom not to expose everybody.

Trust God for your healing, and call for the elders of the church to come to your home and anoint you with oil in the name of the Lord (James 5:14). If your faith is strong and you are healed, then come right on to church. But if for some reason you do not receive your healing, it is the part of wisdom to stay home until you cannot infect others. All this is just loving your "weaker" brother as yourself.

•••••••••••

Physical Demonstrations in Church

QUESTION:

Why is it that some evangelists emphasize the necessity of certain demonstrations as almost necessary to be saved? One will say if you don't shout you are backslidden. Another will try to get people to run the aisles, or to dance. Another evangelist will try to get everybody to jump, quoting (or misquoting) the verse of Scripture, "Jump for joy." This they call "yielding to the Spirit" or "worship." I personally feel that true worship is loving Jesus and moving as He directs, and everybody will not be moved the same way, but will do as I Corinthians 14:26 says. I find very

264

little in the New Testament of apostles urging the people to indulge in physical demonstrations. Don't we have the cart before the horse?

ANSWER:

I can understand why evangelists desire a high level of emotion and excitement in their meetings. Further, many of God's people have become very stiff and formal and starchy in their worship, and they need to be jarred loose and to move out in worship.

Ministers often get frustrated with the coldness and deadness of people claiming to be Pentecostal or Apostolic. This is not a new problem.

My mother gave me an old Methodist book nearly 115 years old entitled *Perfect Love, or Plain Things for Those Who Need Them* by J. A. Wood, which was given to her father by his mother, my great-grandmother. One chapter asks the question, "Does the Bible countenance shouting and praising the Lord with a loud voice?" This old-time Methodist author answers:

*The Bible says, "Let the inhabitants of the rock sing, let them shout from the top of the mountains." I do not know how some of our modern lovers of good order will like this, but it is permission to shout from head-quarters. God says, "Let the villages that Kedar doth inhabit lift up their voices." And, "Let them shout from the top of the mountains." He does not say **when** these poor sons of the desert shall hear the joyful news of the Savior's life, death, and resurrection, and get their wandering feet on the Rock of Ages; but He gives permission when it does take place,* *and their hearts begin to dilate with love to the Lord Jesus, to shout.*

I do not advocate the doctrine that all people must shout. I only say as God says, "Let the inhabitants of the rock shout." Who has authority to stop them? Soldiers shout, sailors shout, politicians shout, and the angels shout, and why may not the Christian shout? Has he no cause to shout?

There is a beautiful variety in the natural world—mountains and valleys, the gentle breeze and the sweeping tornado, sunbeams and the flashes of lightning, the singing of birds and the rolling of thunder.

There is just as great a variety in the spiritual world. When the grace of God reaches some hearts it will show its power by shouts of victory. Some will weep, some will laugh, some will leap, and some will feel so quiet they will hardly want to breathe. There is a great variety of operations by the same Spirit, and all our conventionalities must give way to the will and power of God. We cannot work by an iron rule in praising God.

Amen, my dear Methodist brother!

But while I am 100% for demonstration, worship, and manifestation of the Spirit of all kinds, I have at time witnessed unwise efforts by young evangelists to get people to demonstrate physically, not as an act of worship to God by a loving and surrendered heart, but simply to make noise and commotion for noise and commotion's sake, to key people up to a pitch of excitement.

This kind of "worship" is as meaningless as though the people were yelling "applesauce"! I am sure that the evangelist thought that the meeting was a great success because they had a mighty physical demonstration. And oftentimes the preaching of the Word is relegated to a secondary or unimportant place.

This "evangelist" has become a cheerleader, and his "ministry" is that of whipping up the emotions, emphasizing the effect instead of the cause. "To shout," say they, "is the goal to be achieved. When that is done we have achieved our purpose." How immature and shortsighted!

We should give Jesus to the people, let them behold Him, present them with His beauty, His purity, His power. Let them become enraptured with Him. Then the shouts will come. There will be dancing, worshiping, adoration. We will not have to emphasize the physical aspect so much if we properly and faithfully emphasize the spiritual. Physical demonstrations will flow out of hearts enraptured by Jesus!

If we are apostolic we will obey the apostle's injunction to "preach the word" (II Timothy 4:2). The proper kind of spirit-anointed preaching of the Word of God will move people to worship, not with self-conscious imitations of a certain recommended procedure, or according to directions suggested from the pulpit, but by the moving of the Holy Ghost on loving hearts completely yielded to the Spirit. Only thus shall we ever achieve God's highest and best and wholly acceptable-to-God worship, that which is "in Spirit and in truth, for the Father seeketh such to worship him" (John 4:23).

•••••••••••

Tongues and Interpretation

QUESTION:

I am puzzled over tongues and interpretations. Are there to be no more than three messages in a service, or can there be several groups of three messages each? If one can control the speaking forth in tongues, how can it be a supernatural gift of God? Does the same person (who has the gift of interpretation) interpret all messages? If a message in tongues is not interpreted, could there be another message in tongues come forth which may be interpreted? Does the interpretation to be genuine need to be approximately the same length as the message in tongues? I hope you can help me and other young people (and some not so young) with these questions.

ANSWER:

I hope that I can contribute something to your understanding of a subject that is very dear to the hearts of Pentecostals. We may not all agree on all the points raised by your questions, but I do think mature consideration should be given to this matter and to the exercise of the gifts of the Spirit, so vital in our churches.

Let us look at some of the verses of Scripture relative to the operation of the gifts of tongues and the interpretation of tongues, found in I Corinthians 14.

Verse 12 tells us that we should seek to excel in the use of spiritual gifts for the purpose of edifying or building up the church. If the church is not edified or blessed by the operation of the gifts, then there is something wrong with the way the gifts are used.

Verse 13 says that the one bringing forth the message in tongues should pray that he also may be used to bring the interpretation. This lets us know that no one person has a monopoly on either the exercise of the gift of tongues or the gift of interpretation. God can use various individuals in either of these operations, for He gives to each man "severally as He will" (I Corinthians 12:11).

Verse 23 instructs us that order should prevail, that there should not be tongues continuing on in the church service without interpretation.

Verse 27 gives the instruction that messages in tongues, together with interpretation, should be limited to two or three. "By course" simply means that only one individual is to speak at a time (Gr. *ana meros,* "by turn" or "in turn"—*Vine*).

Verse 28 admonishes us concerning the over-zeal of some who may insist on bringing message after message in tongues, even when there is no interpretation. If a message is not interpreted, there should be no more speaking in tongues.

Verse 32 informs us that those who insist they cannot hold back from speaking forth in tongues, even though it may be contrary to the directions of God's Word, are mistaken. Verse 28 says that if the message is not interpreted, the one exercising the gift of tongues is to speak to himself and to God in silence. This could not be done if verse 32 does not mean what it says. Remember, God never insists on over-riding our own spirits. If your gift is of God, it is subject to the control of your own spirit.

It is important also to realize that the length of the message in tongues and the interpretation do not have to coincide. As a matter of fact, it may take several words in English to properly interpret one word in a foreign or unknown tongue, and the reverse may also be true. A case in point is found in Daniel 5:25-28, where each word of the unknown language meant a full sentence when translated: it took eight words to interpret *Mene,* ten to give the meaning of *Tekel,* and eleven for *Peres.* Jesus cried out four words on the cross, "Eli, Eli, lama sabachthani?" yet it took nine English words to translate.

In closing, let me say that these precious, supernatural gifts which God uses in such wonderful ways to bless the church have been misused and cheapened by some who are overzealous and ignorant of the Scriptures, or by others who take the sacred things of God and prostitute them to their own ends. But this should not discourage us from the use of them in ways that God authorizes which edify and bless the church as nothing else can. Let us covet earnestly the best gifts (I Corinthians 12:31), for the church cannot be spiritually healthy without them.

Finally, the words of the Apostle Paul in the latter verses of I Corinthians 14 sum up the matter:

> *"If any man think himself to be a prophet, or spiritual, let him acknowledge that the things that I write unto you are the commandments of the Lord. But if any man be ignorant, let him be ignorant. Wherefore, brethren, covet to prophesy, and forbid not to speak with tongues. Let all things be done decently and in order" (I Corinthians 14:37-40).*

Let everybody say, Amen!

Weak Christians Using Gifts of the Spirit

QUESTION:

I have noticed at times a person can give a message in tongues and it be interpreted and seemingly witnessed by the Spirit and even by the pastor, and this person is very weak. Why is it?

ANSWER:

Always remember God is sovereign. He can use a donkey, a rooster, a fish, and some people. Why should you think it strange when God uses another individual that you may deem weaker than yourself? In God's eyes your self-righteousness may be worse than their weakness!

It is really not due to a person's holiness or spiritual attainments that God is able to use him. Peter plainly declared that the healing of the lame man was not owing to any super spirituality which he possessed. He asked the people, "Why look ye so earnestly on us, as though by our own power or holiness we had made this man to walk?" (Acts 3:12). So the exercise of a spiritual gift does not establish that individual as necessarily a spiritual person.

On the other hand, we must understand that it is not because of his weaknesses that God uses a person; it is perhaps because He cannot get anyone else to yield to His Spirit. God is looking for someone He can use. So that He may receive all the glory it often pleases God to use weak vessels.

"Not many wise men after the flesh, not many mighty, not many noble, are called: But God hath chosen the foolish things of the world to confound the wise; and God hath chosen the weak things of the world to confound the things which are mighty; And base things of the world, and things which are despised, hath God chosen, yea, and things which are not, to bring to nought things that are: That no flesh should glory in His presence" (I Corinthians 1:26-29).

•••••••••••

"I Have the Gift of Discernment"

QUESTION:

God has given me the gift of discernment, although I seldom say anything because when I do I am criticized. But when I meet a person I can tell right off if he or she is a real Christian or a hypocrite, or if he has a devil. There are some in the church who take an active part, even some of the leaders, who God has revealed to me are hypocrites. What should I do? Should I tell the pastor? He thinks they are wonderful, spiritual people. But I know they will cause trouble later on.

ANSWER:

Frankly, I think you are conceited and self-exalted, and that your "gift of discernment" is very probably the "gift of suspicion." Instead of it coming from God, it originates in your carnal, deceived mind. The Bible calls it "wicked imaginations," and tells us that God hates the heart that devises these thoughts (Proverbs 6:18). If you do not beware, you will soon indulge in other things that God hates, "feet that be swift in running to mischief" and "hands that shed innocent blood." This is quickly followed by "a false witness that speaketh lies, and he that soweth discord among brethren" (Proverbs 6:17-19). This is the way you are headed, and God hates every one of these things.

The gifts of the Spirit are resident, not in the individual, but in the Holy Ghost. The Holy Ghost called your pastor to fill the pastoral office, not you, and in the Holy Ghost he has all he needs to fulfill the place to which God has called him, including discernment as it is needed.

It is unwise for you to claim any gift. The only gift I claim is the gift of the Holy Ghost, although the Holy Ghost has operated many of the gifts of the Spirit through me as the need arose for them. However, they are not mine, and the gift of discernment or any other gift is not yours. It belongs to the Holy Ghost, and He operates the gifts through the one He has called to fulfill the office needing the gift and at the time it is needed. It is not given to the individual to operate at his own will.

Great havoc has been wrought in the church by people claiming to possess certain gifts. I would rather submit myself to a God-called minister who oversees the use of the gifts in the fear of the Lord than to claim to have and try to operate a gift on my own.

A final word to you. You need this "gift" like you need another hole in your head. That is one very solid reason why I know that it is not from God. It does not edify the church; in fact, in your hands it desires to tear the church up. I can but repeat the words of Peter to Simon Magus when he wanted to obtain a gift from Peter to operate on his own:

> *"Repent, therefore, of this thy wickedness, and pray God, if perhaps the thought of thine heart may be forgiven thee; For I perceive that thou art in the gall of bitterness, and in the bond of iniquity" (Acts 8:22-23).*
>
> *"Pray ye to the Lord for me, that none of these things which ye have spoken come upon me" (Acts 8:24).*

The Communion Service

QUESTION:

What exactly does Communion do for the saint? Many saints tell me it does for the saint what baptism does for the sinner. Your comment would be very helpful.

ANSWER:

The Communion service is a memorial of Jesus' death. Jesus said, "This is my body" and "This is my blood"; that is, the emblems of the fruit of the vine and the unleavened bread represent Jesus' body that was broken and His blood that was shed at Calvary. Jesus told us to partake of them "in remembrance of me."

This helps us to understand that as we remember His death on Calvary we are brought close to Him, and by faith we are enabled to appropriate to ourselves that which He purchased for us there.

Many people have been healed during a Communion service when by faith they saw His body which was beaten with stripes and remembered the promise, "By His stripes we are healed." Partaking of the Communion service enabled their faith to rise and appropriate the promise to themselves.

Others have not only reached out for forgiveness and received it, but have also claimed the power of His blood and His name into their lives over weaknesses of the flesh that had defeated them before. It was not the wine or the bread that brought these blessings to them; simply that they "remembered Jesus" in His atoning death, and their faith reached out to grasp the wonderful promises of healing, forgiveness, virtue, and power. These became theirs as they partook of the emblems of the Lord's Supper in obedience to the Word of God.

I do not believe there is automatic virtue or blessing to be gained from partaking of the Lord's Supper; it must be accompanied by other things such as faith and surrender. Always remember that to be able to receive blessing one must "examine himself, and so let him eat of this bread and drink of this cup." It is self-examination together with the Communion that brings God's blessing into your life.

The Lord's Supper helps us remember Calvary and what Jesus did for us there. Then faith reaches out to appropriate the promises of God purchased for us by the broken body and shed blood of the Lamb of God.

At your next Communion service, remember Jesus' death, examine yourself, then actively by faith claim the wonderful promises and blessings Jesus purchased for us in His atonement. You will find that the Communion of the Lord's Supper can be one of the most blessed experiences of your life.

• • • • • • • • • • • •

The Footwashing Service

QUESTION:

We never had Footwashing in the church that I came from, but the pastor of the church I now attend stresses that we have Footwashing at least once a year. Is it necessary?

ANSWER:

Let us first read the scriptural record. It is found in John, chapter 13:

> "*He riseth from supper, and laid aside his garments; and took a towel, and girded himself. After that he poureth water into a bason, and began to wash the disciples' feet, and to wipe them with the towel wherewith he was girded*" *(verses 4-5).*
> "*So after he had washed their feet, and had taken his garments, and was set down again, he said unto them, Know ye what I have done to you?*

Ye call me Master and Lord; and ye say well; for so I am. If I then, your Lord and Master, have washed your feet; ye also ought to wash one another's feet. For I have given you an example, that ye should do as I have done to you" (verses 12-15).

"If you know these things, happy are ye if ye do them" (verse 17).

Jesus let it be known that washing one another's feet was not to be terminated with His doing it, but was to continue and be practiced by His followers.

There are certain things that Footwashing teaches us, which make the practice of this divine institution extremely important to us. First, let us notice that there are three cleansings of which the Bible speaks.

1. There is the cleansing which only Christ can do (Isaiah 1:18; I John 1:7). This cleansing is symbolized by the emblems of the Lord's Supper, instituted by our Lord at the same time as He instituted Footwashing.

2. There is the cleansing of self (II Corinthians 7:1; James 4:8). This cleansing is always to be practiced when we come to partake of the Lord's Supper (I Corinthians 11:28-31), as well as other times.

3. There is the cleansing of one another. (Galatians 6:1, 2; Ephesians 4:32; Colossians 3:13). This is taught by the Footwashing service (John 13:14-15) which Jesus instituted to help us with this cleansing, just as He instituted the Lord's Supper to help us with the first two cleansings.

Jesus said in John 13:10, "He that is washed needeth not save to wash his feet." The thought here is that those who have been washed at the bathhouse do not need to take another full bath after they have walked home. All they need to do is wash their feet that became soiled in the dust of the pathway. So we that have had the cleansing of God through repentance, baptism in Jesus' name, and the Holy Ghost (I Corinthians 6:11) now are walking through this world on our way to our heavenly home, and periodically need our feet washed. We do this both spiritually and literally, just as the Lord's Supper is taken both spiritually and literally. And by doing so we are kept clean and ready for the Rapture.

Any church which does not practice Footwashing, which symbolizes this cleansing, violates the divine plan, and the saints are proportionately weaker. The Footwashing service itself produces such unity and blessing that once it is put into practice, any church will realize the need for it and desire to continue.

Jesus said, concerning Communion and Footwashing, "Happy are ye if you do them" (John 13:17).

• • • • • • • • • • •

Drinking Water When Fasting

QUESTION:

Should a person drink or not drink water when they fast?

ANSWER:

I have always felt, especially in the case of an extended fast, that the drinking of water is permissible. Water has no nourishing value whatsoever, does not stimulate, and simply prevents your body from dehydrating. Water assists the body in cleansing itself of poisons and wastes, which is one of the positive beneficial by-products of fasting.

Neither fruit juice nor soft drinks, coffee or tea should be used while fasting. These either provide nourishment or artificially stimulate the body, and thus destroy the divine purpose which God has in mind for you when you fast.

However, there may be reasons why your pastor may desire you to abstain from water during a short fast. Always go according to your pastor's instructions concerning matters of this nature.

•••••••••••

7

Indexes

Subject Index

Index

Index of Scripture References

Index